# Writing Grade 2

Best Value Books

## Table of Contents

The student pages in this book have been specially prepared for reproduction on any standard copying machine.

Permission is hereby granted to the purchaser of this book to reproduce student pages for classroom use only. Reproduction for commercial resale or for an entire school or school system is strictly prohibited. No part of this book may be reproduced for storage in _____ _____ or transmitted in any form, by any _____, mechanical, or other- ____ permission of the pub-

Kelley Wingate products are available at fine educational supply stores throughout the U.S. and Canada.

D1402833

**Writing Grade 2 KW**       Printed in the United States o. ____       ISBN 0-88724-435-1

# A NOTE TO PARENTS AND TEACHERS

Children are natural storytellers. Most of them can hardly wait to recount their experiences to their teacher or friends. An important task of the parent and teacher is to turn these storytellers into story writers. Children who begin to write early become comfortable with the process. Writing becomes as natural as speaking. It is important to make writing a part of the daily schedule.

Many children find writing difficult because they do not understand how to write. They do not even know how to begin. Any writing activity must be modeled by the teacher several times before a child can grasp the concepts. To achieve the greatest affect, the activity should be conducted with a group. This allows the free exchange of ideas and prompts deeper thinking that will assist in better clarity and comprehension of the concepts. When the task is fully understood and mastered within groups, individual assignments become appropriate.

Writing is a process, and it takes time to develop ideas into a finished product. Neither the teacher nor student should expect a well designed story to emerge from an initial attempt. Teachers and students should look upon writing as a five step process. The first step is gathering ideas pertaining to the writing assignment. The second step is selecting and organizing those ideas into a rough draft. Third is the revising step to reorganize content and refine wording. The fourth step is editing (proofreading) for grammar, capitalization, and punctuation errors. Lastly, the paper is rewritten as a final copy. Remember to use these five steps to guide the writing process.

Students do willingly what they do well. Direct instruction, ample opportunities to practice skills, and exciting topics will support these storytellers in our quest to make them story writers.

## About the author...

During her many years as an educator, **Rae Anne Roberson** has taught in elementary, junior and senior high, and university level settings. She is currently the Title 1 Instructional Facilitator in her school system and is helping to develop several innovative reading programs for "at risk" students in elementary schools. Rae Anne is very active as a presenter at workshops for teachers and parents. She was recently presented with the "Award for Literacy" for her school system. Certified in elementary and secondary education as well as reading specialist, Rae Anne holds an M.Ed. and is currently working toward her doctorate.

**Senior Editors:** Patricia Pedigo and Roger DeSanti
**Production Supervisor:** Homer Desrochers
**Production:** Arlene Evitts and Debra Ollier

# Ready-To-Use Ideas and Activities

The activities in this book will help students master the basic skills necessary to become competent writers. Remember as you read through the activities listed below, and as you go through this book, that all children learn at their own rate. Although repetition is important, it is critical that we never lose sight of the fact that it is equally important to build children's self-esteem and self-confidence if we want them to become successful learners as well as good citizens.

If you are working with a child at home, try to set up a quiet comfortable environment where you will work. Make it a special time to which you each look forward. Do only a few activities at a time. Try to end each session on a positive note, and remember that fostering self-esteem and self-confidence are also critical to the learning process.

The back of this book has removable flash cards that will be great for use for basic skill and vocabulary enrichment activities. Pull the flash cards out and either cut them apart or, if you have access to a paper cutter, use that to cut the flash cards apart.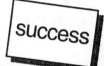

Explain the connection between the spoken and written word by asking a student to tell you what he or she did last weekend. Write the story on a large sheet of chart paper or on the chalkboard. point out the beginning, middle, and end of the story as well as the punctuation.

I had a fun weekend. My sister and I went to the zoo. We saw many different kinds of animals. My sister fed some of the animals. We had lunch and then we played on the slide. We went home at 3:00.

# Ready-To-Use Ideas and Activities

Expose your students to the many types of writing that are out in the world. Newspapers, magazines, advertisements, weather forecasts, recipes, poems, automotive manuals, short stories, novels, personal letters, and more.

Each child will bring his or her own unique background and perspective to the writing task and will, therefore, produce unpredictable responses. However, each written task does require that certain elements be present for the exercise to be correctly completed. Application of guidelines below will be necessary for accurate grading or interpretation of the written responses.

There are two perspectives from which the adult may choose to assess written assignments: content and mechanics. Content assessment takes a look at what the child has written with a focus on the intended message. Mechanics assessment gives attention to capitalization, punctuation, indentation, spelling, grammar, and format of the written piece.

## CONTENT ASSESSMENT CHECKLIST

Does the story follow a logical sequence?
Does the story stick to the topic?
Has the child incorporated the selected key words from the web or story box?
Are adjectives used appropriately to help describe the topic?
Does the story present a clear idea or theme?
Does the story have a beginning, middle and end?

## MECHANICS ASSESSMENT CHECKLIST

Are capitals used at the beginning of each sentence?
Are capitals used for all proper nouns?
Has proper punctuation been used (periods or question marks)?
Is each paragraph indented?
Is a title included when appropriate?
Has the child used correct or inventive spellings?
Has the child printed legibly?
Has the assignment been completed in a manner consistent with the given format (sentence, paragraph, invitation, etc.)?

# Ready-To-Use Ideas and Activities

Reproduce the bingo sheet included in this book, making enough to have one for each student. Hand them out to the students. Take the flash cards and write the words on the chalkboard. Have the students choose 24 of the words and write them in any order on the empty spaces of their bingo cards, writing only one word in each space. When all students have finished filling out their bingo cards, take the flash cards and make them in to a deck. Call out the words one at a time. Any student who has a called out word should make an "X" through the word to cross it out. The student who crosses out five words in a row first (horizontally, vertically, or diagonally) wins the game and shouts "BINGO!".

Reproduce this page and make your own bingo game! Use in conjunction with the enclosed flashcards.

# B I N G O

| | | | | |
|---|---|---|---|---|
| | | | | |
| | | | | |
| | | Free! | | |
| | | | | |
| | | | | |

© 1996 Kelley Wingate Publications CD-3717

Name_____

## Choose a sentence and write a story about it.

Red and yellow leaves ...     Jumping rope...     Mondays are...

Apples taste...     Summer was a ...     Let's go outside and...

I like pizza with lots...     Splash! The frog...     I like the smell...

Remember to...     My dog barks when ...     I looked up and...

Summer was...     September is...

Monday is...     Can you...

SEPTEMBER

_____

_____

_____

_____

_____

_____

Name_____

## Choose a sentence and write a story about it.

Pumpkins can be ...      I lost my best...      My baby sister ...

The wind blows ...      October means ...      Come with me to ...

Ghosts will...      Mom lets me ...      Last night I...      The school bus...

My red jacket...                                                  A witch rides ...

Let's hide in...                                                  All the leaves...

OCTOBER

_____

_____

_____

_____

_____

_____

_____

The ball game...      Grandma will...      I walk to the ...

**Choose a sentence and write a story about it.**

Thanksgiving is a time when ...          School is fun.  I like...

Cold winds blow and ...     The stars are...     Pumpkin pie tastes...

It is time for bears ...          This old bag...          My friend and I...

I will make sure...          I lost a tooth...          My new coat is...

The trees look...     I can write...     I wish I could...     A squirrel is...

# NOVEMBER

_____

_____

_____

_____

_____

_____

_____

_____

Every Friday...          The Pilgrims came...          Birds are starting...

## Choose a sentence and write a story about it.

Go to sleep early because...                    There are bells on...

It's finally Saturday...        Santa will...        Red and green are...

We light candles...        Did I just hear...        I went shopping...

Candy canes...        That book...            The lights look...

DECEMBER

_____

_____

_____

_____

_____

_____

_____

_____

I will help Dad...        I can't wait until...        My family will go ...

The snowy yard...        At recess time...        My class sang...

© 1996 Kelley Wingate Publications        4

## Choose a sentence and write a story about it.

White snowflakes fell ...      A rabbit ...    Put on mittens and...

In January...          The gray sky looked like...          Our sled...

Thursday will be...         I love to go...          Will you help me...

# JANURY

_____

_____

_____

_____

_____

_____

_____

_____

_____

The party was...      When I got up...        It is too cold to...

Dad took me...        At night the stars...          I can write...

Building two snowmen...              There were tracks in...

## Choose a sentence and write a story about it.

I made a valentine for ...        A rose is...        I lost my new...

February is...        When I am happy I...        My secret friend...

What time will we...        A pink heart...        The ground will...

Candy hearts...        Can you see...        My ice skates are...

A snowball just...        Look at this! ...        My room is...        I sent...

The mailman...        FEBRUARY        One day a...

_____

_____

_____

_____

_____

_____

_____

_____

**Choose a sentence and write a story about it.**

Now is the time to ...     March is...     Robins and squirrels...

Kites are flying...     We pick teams...     The pot of gold...

I ride my bike to...     Wear green...     Little birds try...

Do you want...     Can I have...

# MARCH

_____

_____

_____

_____

_____

_____

_____

_____

_____

_____

The strong wind ...     Ice cream is...     Windy days make...

On Tuesday we will...     I really like...     If I could, I would...

## Choose a sentence and write a story about it.

We will hunt for ...        It is time to plant...        The clouds look...

Butterflies...        The rain is...        These eggs...        Will you go...

### APPLE

_____

_____

_____

_____

_____

_____

_____

_____

_____

_____

This basket is...     My umbrella...   A rainbow...        Good books...

I am ready to...     Puddles are...   A busy bee...       That bush is...

In my garden...              I saw a rabbit...        Lazy ladybugs...

**Choose a sentence and write a story about it.**

| | | |
|---|---|---|
| Our trip to the zoo ... | A dragonfly... | I learned about... |
| May is a good time... | I tripped over... | Tulips and roses... |
| Buds are... | Yesterday I... | I think I am... |

## MAY

_____

_____

_____

_____

_____

_____

_____

_____

| | | |
|---|---|---|
| A cowboy rode... | After the storm... | I get mad when... |
| I found a bag with... | Popcorn... | On the way to school... |

## Choose a sentence and write a story about it.

I have a treehouse ...          This summer...          Warm sunshine...

My desk is...          We went to the park and...          June is...

The teacher said...          After school I...          I feel good about...

I will run...          What will I...          I eat breakfast...          How can I...

The days are...          I think...          This year was...          Did you really...

### JUREN JUNE

_____

_____

_____

_____

_____

_____

_____

_____

_____

_____

Every sentence has a beginning and an end.

## Match the beginnings and endings to make five sentences.

Two yellow ducks          shine in the night.

The boys at the zoo       are fun to read.

The moon and stars        swim in the water.

The happy girl            saw many animals.

Good books                smiled at me.

## Write a beginning for each sentence. Use capitals and end with periods.

1. _____ is fun.

2. _____ like to play.

3. _____ goes to work.

4. _____ wears a hat.

5. _____ on the table.

| Every sentence has a beginning and an end. |
|---|

**Match the beginnings and endings to make five sentences.**

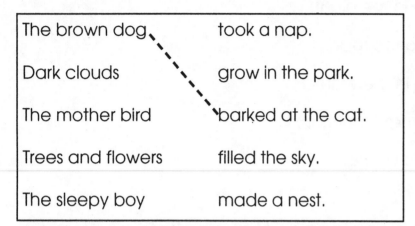

| The brown dog | took a nap. |
| Dark clouds | grow in the park. |
| The mother bird | barked at the cat. |
| Trees and flowers | filled the sky. |
| The sleepy boy | made a nest. |

**Write a beginning for each sentence.  Use capitals and end with periods.**

1. _____ ate his dinner.

2. _____ have four legs.

3. _____ ride my bike.

4. _____ are here.

5. _____ is blue.

© 1996 Kelley Wingate Publications                   CD-3717

Every sentence has a beginning and an end.

**Match the beginnings and endings to make five sentences.**

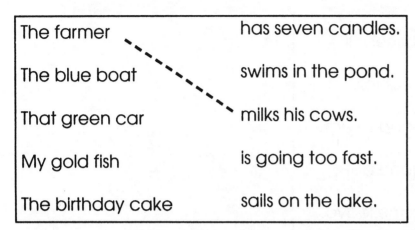

The farmer

The blue boat

That green car

My gold fish

The birthday cake

has seven candles.

swims in the pond.

milks his cows.

is going too fast.

sails on the lake.

**Write an ending for each sentence.  End with a period.**

1. My sister

2. The train

3. My cat

4. The chair

5. Grass is

| Every sentence has a beginning and an end. |

## Match the beginnings and endings to make five sentences.

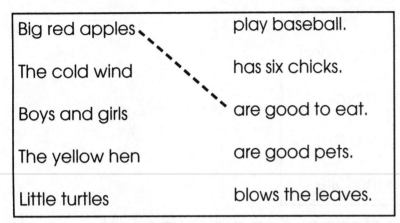

| Big red apples | play baseball. |
| The cold wind | has six chicks. |
| Boys and girls | are good to eat. |
| The yellow hen | are good pets. |
| Little turtles | blows the leaves. |

## Write an ending for each sentence.  End with a period.

1. Her house _____

2. The hot dog _____

3. Five boys _____

4. A big bear _____

5. His nose _____

© 1996 Kelley Wingate Publications          14                      CD-3717

**Every sentence has a beginning and an end.**

## Match the beginnings and endings to make five sentences.

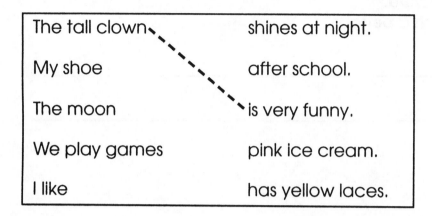

| | |
|---|---|
| The tall clown | shines at night. |
| My shoe | after school. |
| The moon | is very funny. |
| We play games | pink ice cream. |
| I like | has yellow laces. |

## Write five sentences on the lines below.

1. _____

2. _____

3. _____

4. _____

5. _____

| A sentence tells a whole idea. |

**Write a sentence about each picture.**
**Begin with a capital and end with a period.**

shoe _____

_____

soap _____

_____

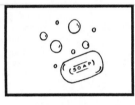

dog _____

_____

girl _____

_____

key _____

_____

| A sentence tells a whole idea. |

**Write a sentence about each picture.**
**Begin with a capital and end with a period.**

train

_____

_____

strawberry

_____

_____

umbrella

_____

_____

vase

_____

_____

walrus

_____

_____

A sentence tells a whole idea.

**Write a sentence about each picture.**
**Begin with a capital and end with a period.**

bike

_____

_____

mop

_____

_____

mouse

_____

_____

pig

_____

_____

sun

_____

_____

## A sentence tells a whole idea.

**Write a sentence about each picture.**
**Begin with a capital and end with a period.**

cabin

_____

_____

airplane

_____

_____

television

_____

_____

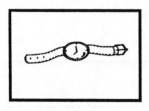

watch

_____

_____

bear

_____

_____

Name_____

## A sentence tells a whole idea.

Write a sentence about each picture.
Begin with a capital and end with a period.

globe

_____

_____

tire

_____

_____

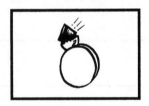

ring

_____

_____

fish

_____

_____

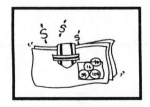

wallet

_____

_____

## Sentences have order

**Unscramble the words to make a sentence.**
**Write the sentence on the line below it.(Put a period at the end.)**

over Summer is

1. _____

in are back We school

2. _____

happy to are here be We

3. _____

will read good We books

4. _____

stories write funny will We

5. _____

all school love We

6. _____

**Write your own sentence about school.**

7. _____

## Sentences have order

**Unscramble the words to make a sentence.**
**Write the sentence on the line below it.(Put a period at the end.)**

red had a Bob balloon

1. _____

got The away balloon

2. _____

after ran He it

3. _____

him came to Tom help

4. _____

tried both catch it They to

5. _____

it They now have

6. _____

**Write your own sentence about a balloon.**

7. _____

© 1996 Kelley Wingate Publications CD-3717

## Sentences have order

**Unscramble the words to make a sentence.**
**Write the sentence on the line below it.(Put a period at the end.)**

named dog My is Fred

1. _____

brown is black He and

2. _____

can He tricks do

3. _____

to sit knows He how

4. _____

over can roll He

5. _____

a good He dog is

6. _____

**Write your own sentence about your pet.**

7. _____

Name_____

## Sentences have order

**Unscramble the words to make a sentence.**
**Write the sentence on the line below it.(Put a period at the end.)**

girls ball The play

1. _____

has Jan bat the

2. _____

ball the She hard hit

3. _____

run make She home a will

4. _____

ball plays Jan well

5. _____

all school love We

6. _____

**Write your own sentence about baseball.**

7. _____

Name_____

| Sentences have order |

**Unscramble the words to make a sentence.**
**Write the sentence on the line below it.(Put a period at the end.)**

in hops bunny A grass the

1. _____

long two has ears He

2. _____

a has He tail white

3. _____

nose His wiggles

4. _____

likes eat to He carrots

5. _____

home him I take will

6. _____

**Write your own sentence about a bunny.**

7. _____

An asking sentence is called a question.  A question ends with a question mark (?).  Words like who, what, where, and when begin questions.

**Write a question about each picture.**
**Begin with a capital and end with a question mark.**

Who _____

_____

egg

What _____

_____

camel

Why _____

_____

drum

Where _____

_____

button

When _____

_____

bell

An asking sentence is called a question. A question ends with a question mark (?). Words like who, what, where, and when begin questions.

**Write a question about each picture.**
**Begin with a capital and end with a question mark.**

calendar

Is
_____
_____

quilt

Are
_____
_____

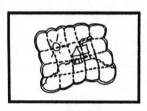

pineapple

Was
_____
_____

mitten

Were
_____
_____

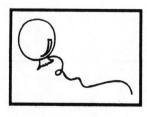

balloon

How
_____
_____

An asking sentence is called a question. A question ends with a question mark (?). Words like who, what, where, and when begin questions.

**Write a question about each picture.**
**Begin with a capital and end with a question mark.**

Did
_____
_____

flowers

Do
_____
_____

snail

May
_____
_____

boy

Can
_____
_____

elephant

Will
_____
_____

crown

An asking sentence is called a question. A question ends with a question mark (?). Words like who, what, where, and when begin questions.

**Write a question about each picture.**
**Begin with a capital and end with a question mark.**

skates

Who
_____
_____

What
_____
_____

cloud

Is
_____
_____

basket

Are
_____
_____

castle

tree

Did
_____
_____

An asking sentence is called a question.  A question ends with a question mark (?).  Words like who, what, where, and when begin questions.

**Write a question about each picture.**
**Begin with a capital and end with a question mark.**

Where
_____
_____

cow

When
_____
_____

frog

Was
_____
_____

ladder

Do
_____
_____

jacket

Can
_____
_____

goat

Telling sentences are called statements.
Asking sentences are called questions.

**Write three statements about the picture.  Use capitals and periods.**

1. _____

2. _____

3. _____

**Write three questions about the picture.  Use capitals and question marks.**

1. _____

2. _____

3. _____

Telling sentences are called statements.
Asking sentences are called questions.

**Write three statements about the picture.  Use capitals and periods.**

1. _____

2. _____

3. _____

**Write three questions about the picture.  Use capitals and question marks.**

1. _____

2. _____

3. _____

Telling sentences are called statements.
Asking sentences are called questions.

**Write three statements about the picture. Use capitals and periods.**

1. _____

2. _____

3. _____

**Write three questions about the picture. Use capitals and question marks.**

1. _____

2. _____

3. _____

Telling sentences are called statements.
Asking sentences are called questions.

**Write three statements about the picture.  Use capitals and periods.**

1. _____

2. _____

3. _____

**Write three questions about the picture.  Use capitals and question marks.**

1. _____

2. _____

3. _____

Telling sentences are called statements.
Asking sentences are called questions.

**Write three statements about the picture.  Use capitals and periods.**

1. _____

2. _____

3. _____

**Write three questions about the picture.  Use capitals and question marks.**

1. _____

2. _____

3. _____

A statement tells you something and ends with a period.
A question asks you something and ends with a question mark.

Write a statement or question about each picture.
Begin with a capital. End with a period or question mark.

apple

_____

_____

flowers

_____

_____

snail

_____

_____

frog

_____

_____

ring

_____

_____

A statement tells you something and ends with a period.
A question asks you something and ends with a question mark.

Write a statement or question about each picture.
Begin with a capital. End with a period or question mark.

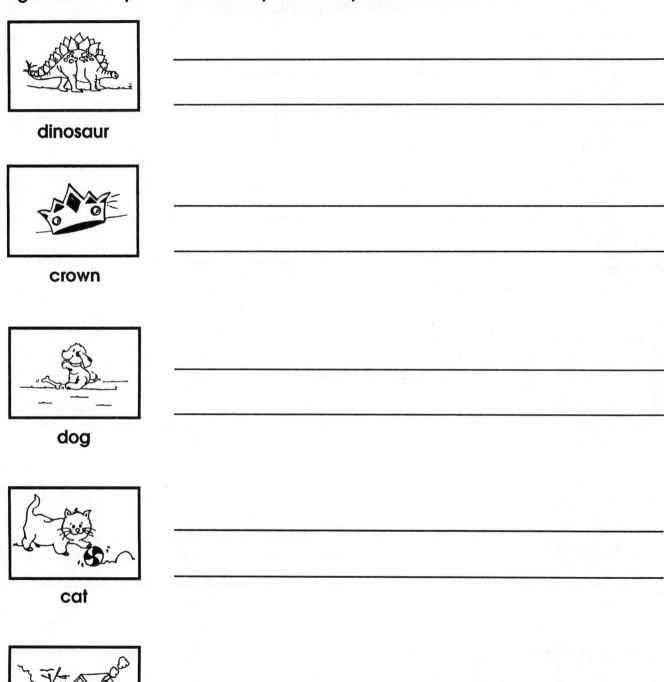

dinosaur

crown

dog

cat

house

| A statement tells you something and ends with a period. |
| A question asks you something and ends with a question mark. |

Write a statement or question about each picture.
Begin with a capital. End with a period or question mark.

train

_____

_____

tire

_____

_____

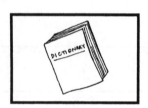

book

_____

_____

tractor

_____

_____

globe

_____

_____

A statement tells you something and ends with a period.
A question asks you something and ends with a question mark.

Write a statement or question about each picture.
Begin with a capital. End with a period or question mark.

bear

_____

_____

watch

_____

_____

toothbrush

_____

_____

girl

_____

_____

airplane

_____

_____

A statement tells you something and ends with a period.
A question asks you something and ends with a question mark.

Write a statement or question about each picture.
Begin with a capital. End with a period or question mark.

shoe

_____

_____

leaf

_____

_____

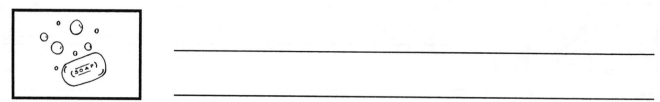
soap

_____

_____

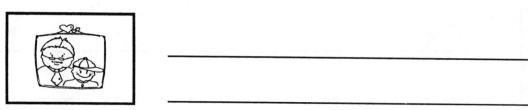
picture

_____

_____

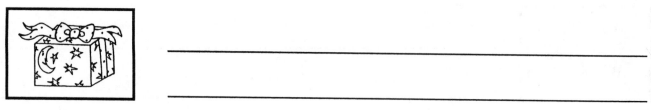
box

_____

_____

A statement tells you something and ends with a period.
A question asks you something and ends with a question mark.

Write a statement or question about each picture.
Begin with a capital. End with a period or question mark.

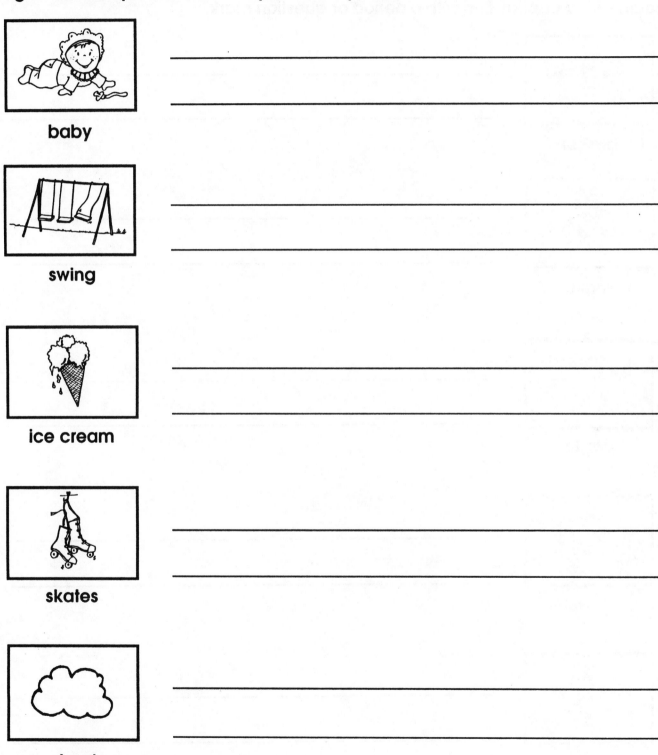

baby

_____

_____

swing

_____

_____

ice cream

_____

_____

skates

_____

_____

cloud

_____

_____

© 1996 Kelley Wingate Publications 41 CD-3717

> A statement tells you something and ends with a period.
> A question asks you something and ends with a question mark.

Write a statement or question about each picture.
Begin with a capital. End with a period or question mark.

basket

_____

_____

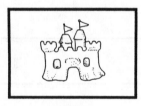

snake

_____

_____

castle

_____

_____

cow

_____

_____

rabbit

_____

_____

A statement tells you something and ends with a period.
A question asks you something and ends with a question mark.

Write a statement or question about each picture.
Begin with a capital. End with a period or question mark.

balloon

_____
_____

crab

_____
_____

circle

_____
_____

tree

_____
_____

elephant

_____
_____

© 1996 Kelley Wingate Publications        43        CD-3717

A statement tells you something and ends with a period.
A question asks you something and ends with a question mark.

Write a statement or question about each picture.
Begin with a capital. End with a period or question mark.

mail

_____

_____

month

_____

_____

radio

_____

_____

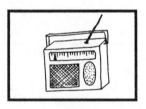

food

_____

_____

television

_____

_____

A statement tells you something and ends with a period.
A question asks you something and ends with a question mark.

Write a statement or question about each picture.
Begin with a capital. End with a period or question mark.

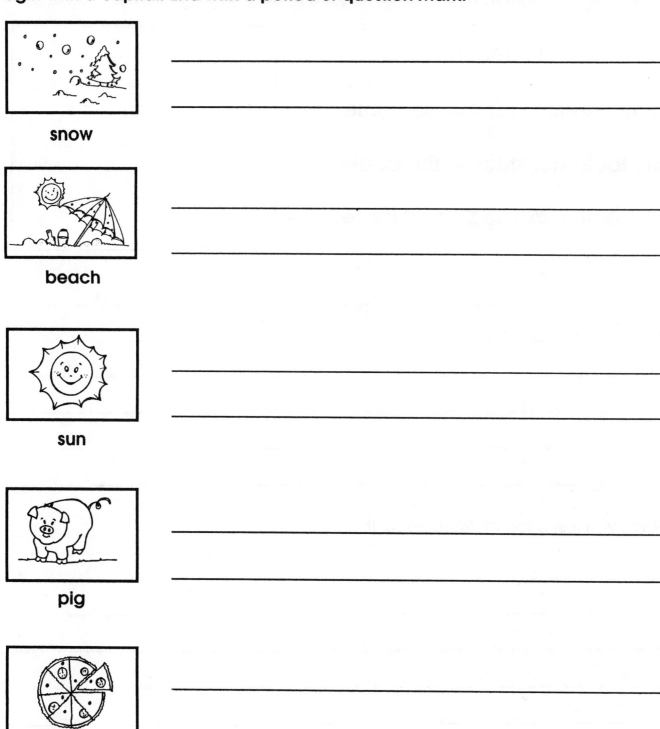

snow

_____

_____

beach

_____

sun

_____

pig

_____

pizza

© 1996 Kelley Wingate Publications          45          CD-3717

| Stories have a beginning, middle, and end. |
|---|

These sentences tell a story.  Write the sentences in order on the lines below.
Be sure to use capitals and periods.  Draw a picture for the story.

### Lost Tooth

During lunch I bit into an apple.

My tooth got stuck in the apple.

My tooth was wiggly and loose.

1. _____

_____

2. _____

_____

3. _____

_____

Have you lost a tooth?  Write about it.

_____

_____

_____

_____

_____

| Stories have a beginning, middle, and end. |

These sentences tell a story.  Write the sentences in order on the lines below.
Be sure to use capitals and periods.  Draw a picture for the story.

### The Cat

She curled up in front of the warm fireplace.

The cat was cold and tired.

The cat fell asleep.

1. _____

   _____

2. _____

   _____

3. _____

   _____

What kind of pet would you like to have?  Write about it.

_____

_____

_____

_____

_____

| Stories have a beginning, middle, and end. |

These sentences tell a story.  Write the sentences in order on the lines below.
Be sure to use capitals and periods.

### A Letter

I wrote a letter to my best friend.

I put the letter into the mailbox.

I licked the envelope and put on a
stamp.

1. _____

_____

2. _____

_____

3. _____

_____

Have you ever gotten mail?  Write about it.

_____

_____

_____

_____

_____

_____

| Stories have a beginning, middle, and end. |
| --- |

These sentences tell a story.  Write the sentences in order on the lines below.
Be sure to use capitals and periods.

## A New Friend

The horse was very big and I was scared!

I gave him a carrot and we became friends.

I went horseback riding last week.

1. _____

_____

2. _____

_____

3. _____

_____

Can you ride a horse?  Write about it.

_____

_____

_____

_____

_____

| Stories have a beginning, middle, and end. |
| --- |

These sentences tell a story.  Write the sentences in order on the lines below.
Be sure to use capitals and periods.

## Baby Chick

There were ten eggs in the warm box.

Out popped a fuzzy baby chick!

Suddenly one egg jiggled and cracked open.

1. _____

   _____

2. _____

   _____

3. _____

   _____

What would you see on a farm?  Write about it.

_____

_____

_____

_____

_____

_____

Name _____

| Stories tell about someone doing something. |

Pictures can tell a story.  Draw a picture of a child who has chicken pox.
Add something of your own to the picture.  Answer the questions about
your "picture story".

1.  Who is this story about? _____

_____

2.  Where does this story take place? _____

_____

3.  What happens first? _____

_____

4.  What happens next? _____

_____

5.  How does the story end? _____

_____

Have you ever been sick?  Write about it.

_____

_____

_____

_____

_____

| Stories tell about someone doing something. |
|---|

Pictures can tell a story. Draw a picture of a snowman. Put a funny hat on his head. Add something of your own to the picture. Answer the questions about your "picture story".

1. Who is this story about? _____

_____

2. Where does this story take place? _____

_____

3. What happens first? _____

_____

4. What happens next? _____

_____

5. How does the story end? _____

_____

What would you do in the snow? Write about it.

_____

_____

_____

_____

_____

> **Stories tell about someone doing something.**

**Pictures can tell a story.  Draw a picture of a birdhouse in a tree.
Add something of your own to the picture.  Answer the questions about
your "picture story".**

```
┌─────────────────────────────────────────────┐
│                                             │
│                                             │
│                                             │
│                                             │
│                                             │
│                                             │
└─────────────────────────────────────────────┘
```

1.  **Who is this story about?** _____

_____

2.  **Where does this story take place?** _____

_____

3.  **What happens first?** _____

_____

4.  **What happens next?** _____

_____

5.  **How does the story end?** _____

_____

**Have you ever watched a bird?  Write about it.**

_____

_____

_____

_____

_____

| Stories tell about someone doing something. |
| --- |

Pictures can tell a story.  Draw a picture of a present with a big bow.
Add something of your own to the picture.  Answer the questions about
your "picture story".

1. Who is this story about? _____

_____

2. Where does this story take place? _____

_____

3. What happens first?  _____

_____

4. What happens next?  _____

_____

5. How does the story end?  _____

_____

What would you like for a present?  Write about it.

_____

_____

_____

_____

_____

> **Stories tell about someone doing something.**

Pictures can tell a story. Draw a picture of a large orange pumpkin still on the vine. Add something of your own to the picture. Answer the questions about your "picture story".

1. **Who is this story about?** _____

_____

2. **Where does this story take place?** _____

_____

3. **What happens first?** _____

_____

4. **What happens next?** _____

_____

5. **How does the story end?** _____

_____

**Do you have a special plant in your home or yard? Write about it.**

_____

_____

_____

_____

_____

_____

| Stories tell about someone doing something. |
|---|

Pictures can tell a story.  Draw a picture of a a magician pulling a rabbit out of a hat.  Add something of your own to the picture.  Answer the questions about your "picture story".

1.  Who is this story about? _____

_____

2.  Where does this story take place? _____

_____

3.  What happens first?  _____

_____

4.  What happens next?  _____

_____

5.  How does the story end?  _____

_____

Have you ever seen a magic show?  Write about it.

_____

_____

_____

_____

_____

| Stories tell about someone doing something. |
| --- |

Pictures can tell a story.  Draw a picture of yourself.  Add something of your own to the picture.  Answer the questions about your "picture story".

1. Who is this story about? _____

_____

2. Where does this story take place? _____

_____

3. What happens first? _____

_____

4. What happens next? _____

_____

5. How does the story end? _____

_____

What is special about you?  Write about it.

_____

_____

_____

_____

_____

| Stories tell about someone doing something. |

Pictures can tell a story.  Draw a picture of your favorite flowers.
Add something of your own to the picture.  Answer the questions about your
"picture story".

```



```

1.  Who is this story about? _____

_____

2.  Where does this story take place? _____

_____

3.  What happens first? _____

_____

4.  What happens next? _____

_____

5.  How does the story end? _____

_____

What are your favorite kind of flowers?  Write about them.

_____

_____

_____

_____

_____

Name _____

| Stories tell about someone doing something. |

Pictures can tell a story.  Draw a picture of a pair of shoes.  Show the laces in bows.  Add something of your own to the picture.  Answer the questions about your "picture story".

1.  Who is this story about? _____

_____

2.  Where does this story take place? _____

_____

3.  What happens first? _____

_____

4.  What happens next? _____

_____

5.  How does the story end? _____

_____

Can you tie your shoes?  Write about it.

_____

_____

_____

_____

_____

© 1996 Kelley Wingate Publications                               CD-3717

Name _____

| Stories tell about someone doing something. |

Pictures can tell a story. Draw a picture of a scary Halloween costume. Add something of your own to the picture. Answer the questions about your "picture story".

1. Who is this story about? _____

_____

2. Where does this story take place? _____

_____

3. What happens first? _____

_____

4. What happens next? _____

_____

5. How does the story end? _____

_____

What were you dressed as last Halloween? Write about it.

_____

_____

_____

_____

_____

© 1996 Kelley Wingate Publications CD-3717

Stories have a beginning, a middle, and an end.

**Word Box**

whale
huge
water
blow
air
tail
grey
fins

_____

_____

_____

_____

_____

_____

_____

**Things to think about:**
Who is this story about?  Where does the story take place?  How does this story begin?
What happens next?  How does the story end?

© 1996 Kelley Wingate Publications
© 1996 Kelley Wingate Publications
CD-3717

Stories have a beginning, a middle, and an end.

**Word Box**

camping
woods
tent
cook
flashlight
fire
sleep
bugs

_____

_____

_____

_____

_____

_____

_____

_____

**Things to think about:**
Who is this story about?  Where does the story take place?  How does this story begin?
What happens next?  How does the story end?

Name _____

| Stories have a beginning, a middle, and an end. |
| --- |

Use the words in the word box to write a story about the picture.
Remember to use capitals and periods.  Make a title for your story.

**Word Box**

skis
mittens
boots
snow
hills
fun
ice
winter

_____

_____

_____

_____

_____

_____

_____

**Things to think about:**
Who is this story about?  Where does the story take place?  How does this story begin?
What happens next?  How does the story end?

© 1996 Kelley Wingate Publications                    CD-3717

Stories have a beginning, a middle, and an end.

Use the words in the word box to write a story about the picture.
Remember to use capitals and periods.  Make a title for your story.

**Word Box**

people
afraid
pray
sing
dance
clap
alone
stage

_____

_____

_____

_____

_____

_____

_____

**Things to think about:**
Who is this story about?  Where does the story take place?  How does this story begin?
What happens next?  How does the story end?

© 1996 Kelley Wingate Publications

CD-3717

| Stories have a beginning, a middle, and an end. |
| --- |

Use the words in the word box to write a story about the picture.
Remember to use capitals and periods. Make a title for your story.

**Word Box**

pool
swim
splash
float
water
diving
towel
jump

_____

_____

_____

_____

_____

_____

_____

**Things to think about:**
Who is this story about?  Where does the story take place?  How does this story begin?
What happens next?  How does the story end?

| Stories have a beginning, a middle, and an end. |
| --- |

Use the words in the word box to write a story about the picture.
Remember to use capitals and periods.  Make a title for your story.

**Word Box**

duck
swim
water
splash
feathers
quack
friends
fun

_____

_____

_____

_____

_____

_____

_____

_____

**Things to think about:**
Who is this story about?  Where does the story take place?  How does this story begin?
What happens next?  How does the story end?

Name _____

| Stories have a beginning, a middle, and an end. |

Use the words in the word box to write a story about the picture.
Remember to use capitals and periods.  Make a title for your story.

**Word Box**

worm
crawl
flowers
happy
slowly
grass
leaves
green

_____

_____

_____

_____

_____

_____

_____

**Things to think about:**
Who is this story about?  Where does the story take place?  How does this story begin?
What happens next?  How does the story end?

Stories have a beginning, a middle, and an end.

Use the words in the word box to write a story about the picture.
Remember to use capitals and periods. Make a title for your story.

**Word Box**

kangaroo
tail
pouch
strong
jump
legs
baby
hop

_____

_____

_____

_____

_____

_____

_____

_____

**Things to think about:**
Who is this story about? Where does the story take place? How does this story begin?
What happens next? How does the story end?

| Stories have a beginning, a middle, and an end. |
| --- |

Use the words in the word box to write a story about the picture.
Remember to use capitals and periods.  Make a title for your story.

**Word Box**

house
bird
fly
tree
food
seed
far
wings

_____

_____

_____

_____

_____

_____

_____

_____

**Things to think about:**
Who is this story about?  Where does the story take place?  How does this story begin?
What happens next?  How does the story end?

Name _____

Stories have a beginning, a middle, and an end.

Use the words in the word box to write a story about the picture.
Remember to use capitals and periods. Make a title for your story.

**Word Box**

ocean
waves
water
octopus
eight
deep
legs
wet

_____

_____

_____

_____

_____

_____

_____

**Things to think about:**

Who is this story about? Where does the story take place? How does this story begin?
What happens next? How does the story end?

© 1996 Kelley Wingate Publications                   CD-3717

| Stories have a beginning, a middle, and an end. |

**Add 5 more words to the word box and use them to write a story about the picture. Remember to use capitals and periods.  Make a title for your story.**

**Word Box**
frog
pond
leap

_____

_____

_____

_____

_____

_____

_____

_____

_____

_____

_____

_____

_____

**Things to think about:**
Who is this story about?  Where does the story take place?  How does this story begin?  What happens next?  How does the story end?

© 1996 Kelley Wingate Publications          71          CD-3717

| Stories have a beginning, a middle, and an end. |
| --- |

**Add 5 more words to the word box and use them to write a story about the picture. Remember to use capitals and periods.  Make a title for your story.**

**Word Box**
ladder
tree
apples

_____

_____

_____

_____

_____

_____

_____

_____

_____

_____

_____

_____

_____

**Things to think about:**
Who is this story about?  Where does the story take place?  How does this story begin?  What happens next?  How does the story end?

Stories have a beginning, a middle, and an end.

**Add 5 more words to the word box and use them to write a story about the picture. Remember to use capitals and periods. Make a title for your story.**

**Word Box**
chair
fell
book

_____

_____

_____

_____

_____

_____

_____

_____

_____

_____

_____

_____

**Things to think about:**
Who is this story about? Where does the story take place? How does this story begin? What happens next? How does the story end?

| Stories have a beginning, a middle, and an end. |
| :---: |

**Add 5 more words to the word box and use them to write a story about the picture. Remember to use capitals and periods. Make a title for your story.**

**Word Box**
giraffe
neck
leaves

_____

_____

_____

_____

_____

_____

_____

_____

_____

_____

_____

_____

_____

**Things to think about:**
Who is this story about? Where does the story take place? How does this story begin? What happens next? How does the story end?

| Stories have a beginning, a middle, and an end. |
| --- |

**Add 5 more words to the word box and use them to write a story about the picture. Remember to use capitals and periods. Make a title for your story.**

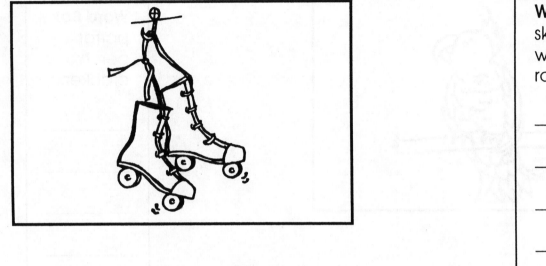

**Word Box**
skates
wheels
roll

_____

_____

_____

_____

_____

_____

_____

_____

_____

_____

_____

_____

_____

**Things to think about:**
Who is this story about?  Where does the story take place?  How does this story begin?  What happens next?  How does the story end?

| Stories have a beginning, a middle, and an end. |
| --- |

**Add 5 more words to the word box and use them to write a story about the picture. Remember to use capitals and periods. Make a title for your story.**

**Word Box**
parrot
perch
cracker

_____

_____

_____

_____

_____

_____

_____

_____

_____

_____

_____

_____

**Things to think about:**
Who is this story about?  Where does the story take place?  How does this story begin?  What happens next?  How does the story end?

| Stories have a beginning, a middle, and an end. |

**Add 5 more words to the word box and use them to write a story about the picture. Remember to use capitals and periods. Make a title for your story.**

**Word Box**
giant
friend
frighten

_____

_____

_____

_____

_____

_____

_____

_____

_____

_____

_____

_____

_____

**Things to think about:**
Who is this story about?  Where does the story take place?  How does this story begin?  What happens next?  How does the story end?

Stories have a beginning, a middle, and an end.

**Add 5 more words to the word box and use them to write a story about the picture. Remember to use capitals and periods. Make a title for your story.**

**Word Box**
sleepy
girl
dream

_____

_____

_____

_____

_____

_____

_____

_____

_____

_____

_____

_____

_____

**Things to think about:**
Who is this story about? Where does the story take place? How does this story begin? What happens next? How does the story end?

© 1996 Kelley Wingate Publications

CD-3717

Stories have a beginning, a middle, and an end.

Add 5 more words to the word box and use them to write a story about the picture. Remember to use capitals and periods. Make a title for your story.

**Word Box**
castle
bridge
moat

_____

_____

_____

_____

_____

_____

_____

_____

**Things to think about:**
Who is this story about? Where does the story take place? How does this story begin? What happens next? How does the story end?

Stories have a beginning, a middle, and an end.

**Add 5 more words to the word box and use them to write a story about the picture.  Remember to use capitals and periods.  Make a title for your story.**

**Word Box**
owl
night
wise

_____

_____

_____

_____

_____

_____

_____

_____

_____

_____

_____

_____

**Things to think about:**
Who is this story about?  Where does the story take place?  How does this story begin?  What happens next?  How does the story end?

© 1996 Kelley Wingate Publications             CD-3717

Name _____

| Stories have a beginning, a middle, and an end. |
| --- |

**Use the words in the story web to write a story about the picture. Remember to use capitals and periods. Make a title for your story.**

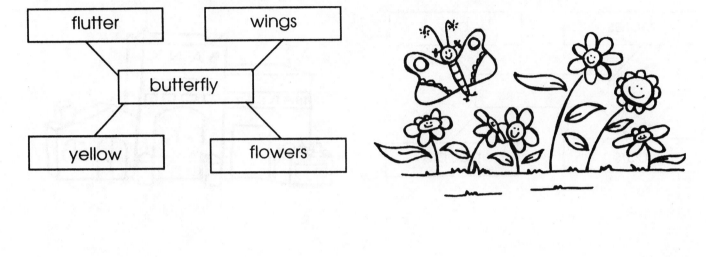

_____

_____

_____

_____

_____

_____

_____

**Things to think about:**
Who is this story about? Where does the story take place? How does this story begin? What happens next? How does the story end?

Stories have a beginning, a middle, and an end.

**Use the words in the story web to write a story about the picture.**
**Remember to use capitals and periods.  Make a title for your story.**

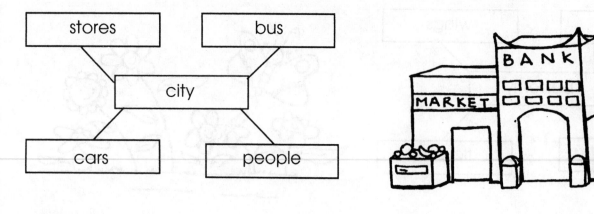

stores

bus

city

cars

people

_____

_____

_____

_____

_____

_____

_____

_____

**Things to think about:**
Who is this story about?  Where does the story take place?  How does this story
begin?  What happens next?  How does the story end?

| Stories have a beginning, a middle, and an end. |
| --- |

**Use the words in the story web to write a story about the picture. Remember to use capitals and periods. Make a title for your story.**

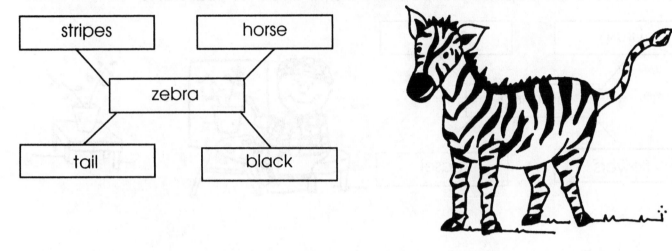

stripes    horse

zebra

tail    black

_____

_____

_____

_____

_____

_____

_____

_____

**Things to think about:**

Who is this story about?  Where does the story take place?  How does this story begin?  What happens next?  How does the story end?

Name _____

Stories have a beginning, a middle, and an end.

**Use the words in the story web to write a story about the picture.
Remember to use capitals and periods. Make a title for your story.**

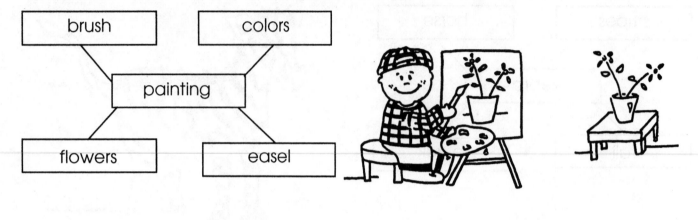

_____

_____

_____

_____

_____

_____

_____

**Things to think about:**
Who is this story about?  Where does the story take place?  How does this story
begin?  What happens next?  How does the story end?

| Stories have a beginning, a middle, and an end. |
| --- |

**Use the words in the story web to write a story about the picture.**
**Remember to use capitals and periods.  Make a title for your story.**

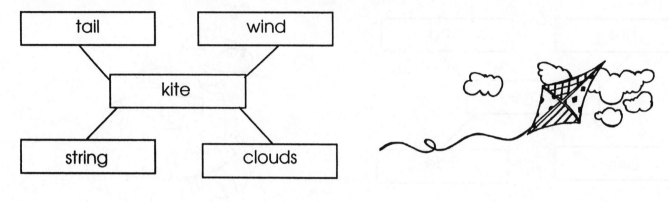

_____

_____

_____

_____

_____

_____

_____

**Things to think about:**
Who is this story about?  Where does the story take place?  How does this story
begin?  What happens next?  How does the story end?

Name _____    Skill: Word Box Story

Stories have a beginning, a middle, and an end.

**Use the words in the story web to write a story about the picture.**
**Remember to use capitals and periods.  Make a title for your story.**

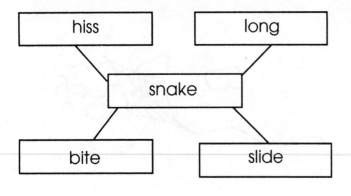

_____

_____

_____

_____

_____

_____

_____

**Things to think about:**
Who is this story about?  Where does the story take place?  How does this story
begin?  What happens next?  How does the story end?

© 1996 Kelley Wingate Publications                    86                    CD-3717

| Stories have a beginning, a middle, and an end. |
| :---: |

**Use the words in the story web to write a story about the picture.**
**Remember to use capitals and periods. Make a title for your story.**

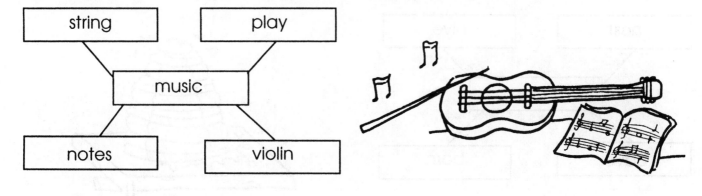

_____

_____

_____

_____

_____

_____

_____

**Things to think about:**
Who is this story about? Where does the story take place? How does this story
begin? What happens next? How does the story end?

| Stories have a beginning, a middle, and an end. |

**Use the words in the story web to write a story about the picture.**
**Remember to use capitals and periods. Make a title for your story.**

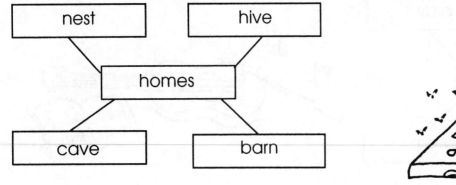

_____

_____

_____

_____

_____

_____

_____

_____

**Things to think about:**
Who is this story about?  Where does the story take place?  How does this story
begin?  What happens next?  How does the story end?

| Stories have a beginning, a middle, and an end. |
|---|

**Use the words in the story web to write a story about the picture.**
**Remember to use capitals and periods. Make a title for your story.**

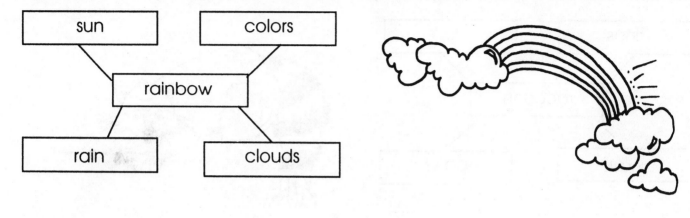

_____

_____

_____

_____

_____

_____

_____

**Things to think about:**
Who is this story about? Where does the story take place? How does this story begin? What happens next? How does the story end?

| Stories have a beginning, a middle, and an end. |

**Use the words in the story web to write a story about the picture.**
**Remember to use capitals and periods. Make a title for your story.**

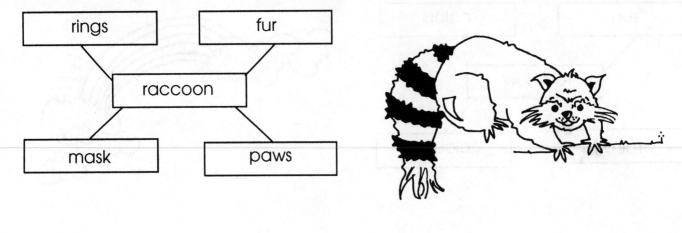

| rings |   | fur |
| mask |   | paws |

raccoon

_____

_____

_____

_____

_____

_____

_____

_____

**Things to think about:**
Who is this story about? Where does the story take place? How does this story
begin? What happens next? How does the story end?

| Stories have a beginning, a middle, and an end. |
| --- |

**Finish the story web then use the words to write a story about the picture. Remember to use capitals and periods. Make a title for your story.**

| teacher | | |
| --- | --- | --- |

school

_____

_____

_____

_____

_____

_____

_____

_____

## Things to think about:

Who is this story about?  Where does the story take place?  How does this story begin?
What happens next?  How does the story end?

Stories have a beginning, a middle, and an end.

**Finish the story web then use the words to write a story about the picture. Remember to use capitals and periods. Make a title for your story.**

bunny

spring

_____

_____

_____

_____

_____

_____

_____

_____

**Things to think about:**
Who is this story about?  Where does the story take place?  How does this story begin?
What happens next?  How does the story end?

Stories have a beginning, a middle, and an end.

**Finish the story web then use the words to write a story about the picture. Remember to use capitals and periods. Make a title for your story.**

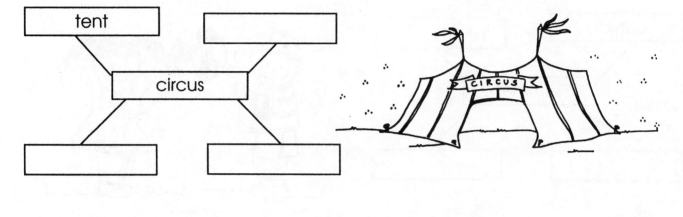

_____

_____

_____

_____

_____

_____

_____

**Things to think about:**

Who is this story about?  Where does the story take place?  How does this story begin?
What happens next?  How does the story end?

Name_____

Stories have a beginning, a middle, and an end.

**Finish the story web then use the words to write a story about the picture. Remember to use capitals and periods. Make a title for your story.**

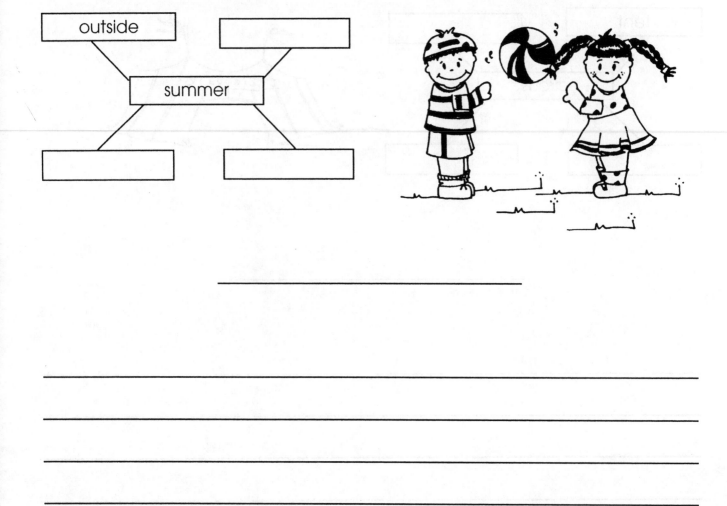

_____

_____

_____

_____

_____

_____

_____

_____

**Things to think about:**

Who is this story about?  Where does the story take place?  How does this story begin?
What happens next?  How does the story end?

© 1996 Kelley Wingate Publications          94

| Stories have a beginning, a middle, and an end. |

**Finish the story web then use the words to write a story about the picture. Remember to use capitals and periods. Make a title for your story.**

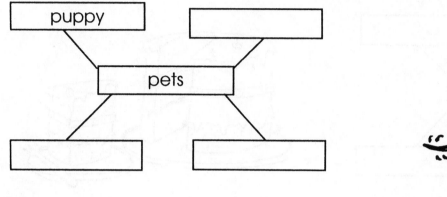

puppy

pets

_____

_____

_____

_____

_____

_____

_____

**Things to think about:**
Who is this story about?  Where does the story take place?  How does this story begin?
What happens next?  How does the story end?

Stories have a beginning, a middle, and an end.

**Finish the story web then use the words to write a story about the picture. Remember to use capitals and periods.  Make a title for your story.**

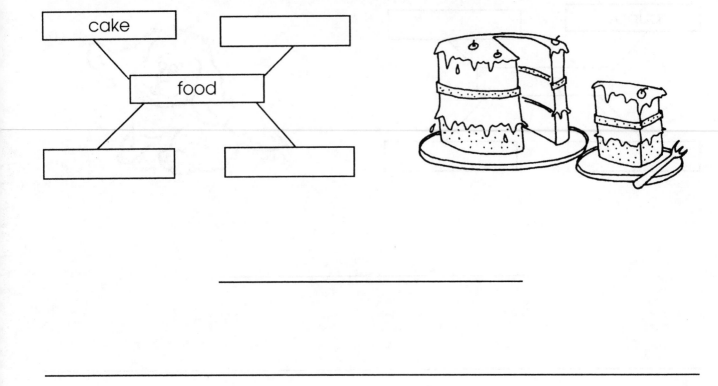

cake

food

_____

_____

_____

_____

_____

_____

_____

**Things to think about:**
Who is this story about?  Where does the story take place?  How does this story begin?
What happens next?  How does the story end?

Stories have a beginning, a middle, and an end.

**Finish the story web then use the words to write a story about the picture.
Remember to use capitals and periods.  Make a title for your story.**

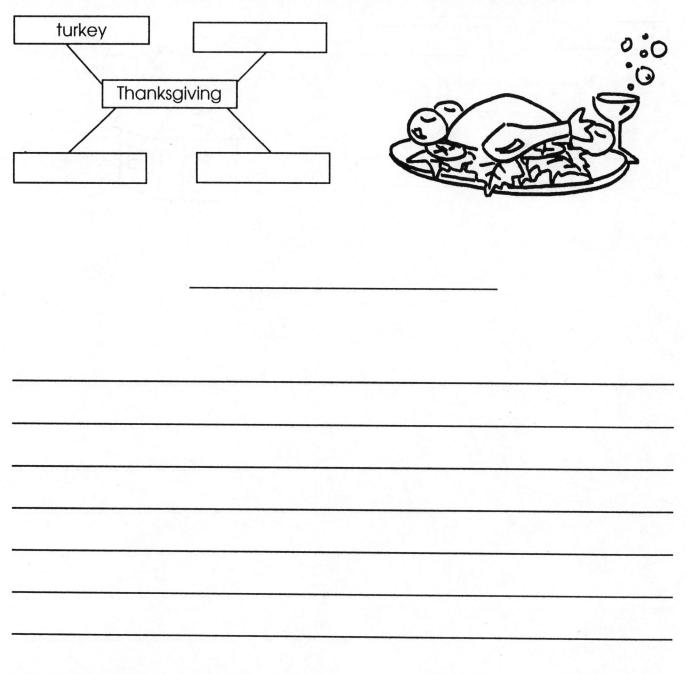

| turkey | | |
|---|---|---|

Thanksgiving

_____

_____

_____

_____

_____

_____

_____

**Things to think about:**
Who is this story about?  Where does the story take place?  How does this story begin?
What happens next?  How does the story end?

Stories have a beginning, a middle, and an end.

**Finish the story web then use the words to write a story about the picture. Remember to use capitals and periods. Make a title for your story.**

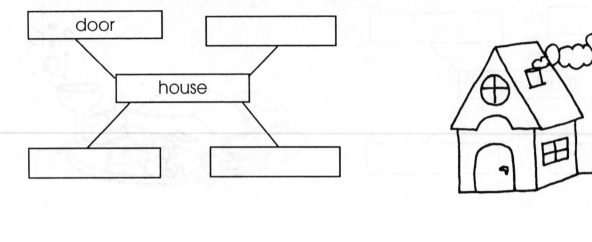

_____

_____

_____

_____

_____

_____

**Things to think about:**
Who is this story about? Where does the story take place? How does this story begin?
What happens next? How does the story end?

Stories have a beginning, a middle, and an end.

**Finish the story web then use the words to write a story about the picture. Remember to use capitals and periods. Make a title for your story.**

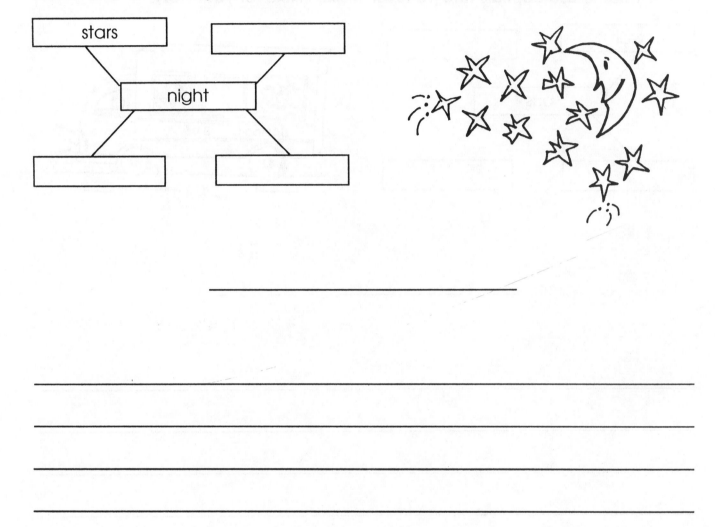

_____

_____

_____

_____

_____

_____

_____

_____

**Things to think about:**
Who is this story about?  Where does the story take place?  How does this story begin?
What happens next?  How does the story end?

Stories have a beginning, a middle, and an end.

**Finish the story web then use the words to write a story about the picture.**
**Remember to use capitals and periods.  Make a title for your story.**

wait

bus

_____

_____

_____

_____

_____

_____

_____

_____

**Things to think about:**
Who is this story about?  Where does the story take place?  How does this story begin?
What happens next?  How does the story end?

© 1996 Kelley Wingate Publications          100          CD-3717

| Stories have a beginning, a middle, and an end. |
| --- |

**Write a story about the picture. Remember to use capitals and periods.
Title your story.**

_____

_____

_____

_____

_____

_____

_____

**Things to think about:**
Who is this story about? Where does the story take place? How does this story
begin? What happens next? How does the story end?

| Stories have a beginning, a middle, and an end. |
| --- |

**Write a story about the picture. Remember to use capitals and periods. Title your story.**

_____

_____

_____

_____

_____

_____

_____

_____

**Things to think about:**
Who is this story about?  Where does the story take place?  How does this story
begin?  What happens next?  How does the story end?

| Stories have a beginning, a middle, and an end. |
| --- |

**Write a story about the picture.  Remember to use capitals and periods. Title your story.**

_____

_____

_____

_____

_____

_____

_____

**Things to think about:**
Who is this story about?  Where does the story take place?  How does this story begin?  What happens next?  How does the story end?

| Stories have a beginning, a middle, and an end. |
| --- |

**Write a story about the picture. Remember to use capitals and periods. Title your story.**

_____

_____

_____

_____

_____

_____

_____

_____

**Things to think about:**
Who is this story about?  Where does the story take place?  How does this story begin?  What happens next?  How does the story end?

© 1996 Kelley Wingate Publications       CD-3717

# Writing Award

_____

**receives this award for**

_____

**Keep up the great work!**

_____

signed

_____

date

# Writing Whiz!

_____

**receives this award for**

_____

Great Job!

_____

signed

_____

date

© 1996 Kelley Wingate Publications

CD-3717

# Wonderful Writing!

_____

receives this award for

_____

## Keep up the great work!

_____   _____
signed                         date

---

# All Star Writer

_____

is a Writing All Star!

_____

## You are terrific!

_____   _____
signed                         date

© 1996 Kelley Wingate Publications          106          CD-3717

# Answer Key

---

Name_____ Skill: Creative Writing – September

**Choose a sentence and write a story about it.**

Red and yellow leaves ...    Jumping rope...    Mondays are...

Apples taste...    Summer was a ...    Let's go outside and...

I like pizza with lots...    Splash! The frog...    I like the smell...

Remember to...    My dog barks when ...    I looked up and...

Summer was...                                September is...

Monday is...                                 Can you...

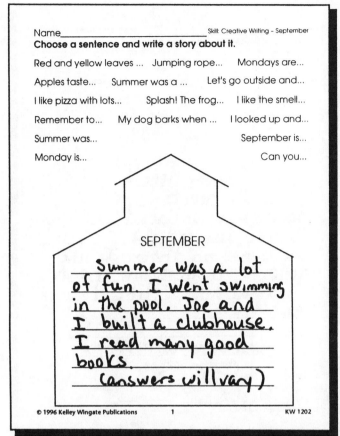

SEPTEMBER

Summer was a lot
of fun. I went swimming
in the pool. Joe and
I built a clubhouse.
I read many good
books.
     (answers will vary)

© 1996 Kelley Wingate Publications        1        KW 1202

---

Name_____ Skill: Creative Writing –October

**Choose a sentence and write a story about it.**

Pumpkins can be ...    I lost my best ...    My baby sister ...

The wind blows ...    October means ...    Come with me to ...

Ghosts will...  Mom lets me ...  Last night I...  The school bus...

My red jacket...                            A witch rides ...

Let's hide in...                            All the leaves...

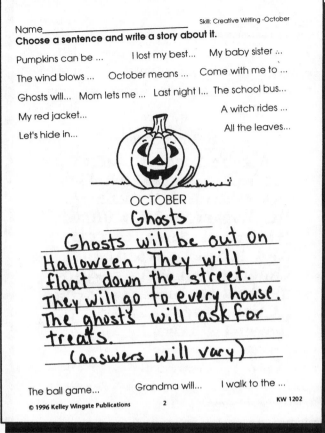

OCTOBER

Ghosts
     Ghosts will be out on
Halloween. They will
float down the street.
They will go to every house.
The ghosts will ask for
treats.
     (answers will vary)

The ball game...        Grandma will...    I walk to the ...

© 1996 Kelley Wingate Publications        2        KW 1202

---

Name_____ Skill: Creative Writing –November

**Choose a sentence and write a story about it.**

Thanksgiving is a time when ...        School is fun.  I like...

Cold winds blow and ...    The stars are...    Pumpkin pie tastes...

It is time for bears ...    This old bag...    My friend and I...

I will make sure...    I lost a tooth...    My new coat is...

The trees look...    I can write...    I wish I could...    A squirrel is...

NOVEMBER

Bare Trees
     The trees look so
bare in November. The
wind has blown their
leaves away. The branches
have nothing to hide
behind. Bare trees look
a little spooky.
     (answers will vary)

Every Friday...    The Pilgrims came...    Birds are starting...

© 1996 Kelley Wingate Publications        3        KW 1202

---

Name_____ Skill: Creative Writing –December

**Choose a sentence and write a story about it.**

Go to sleep early because...              There are bells on...

It's finally Saturday...    Santa will...    Red and green are...

We light candles...    Did I just hear...    I went shopping...

Candy canes...    That book...            The lights look...

DECEMBER

The Present
     I went shopping last
Saturday. I wanted to get
my sister a Christmas
present. I looked for a
long time. I finally
found a present she
will like.
     (answers will vary)

I will help Dad...    I can't wait until...    My family will go ...

The snowy yard...    At recess time...    My class sang...

© 1996 Kelley Wingate Publications        4        KW 1202

---

## JANUARY

Name_____  Skill: Creative Writing -January

**Choose a sentence and write story about it.**

White snowflakes fell ...    A rabbit ...    Put on mittens and...

In January...    The gray sky looked like...    Our sled...

Thursday will be...    I love to go...    Will you help me...

JANUARY

*Rabbit Food*

A rabbit came out of his hole. It was winter. The rabbit was hungry. He hopped into a yard. He found some carrots and lettuce in a dish. Children had left the food for him. He was happy. (answers will vary)

The party was...    When I got up...    It is too cold to...

Dad took me...    At night the stars...    I can write...

Building two snowmen...    There were tracks in...

© 1996 Kelley Wingate Publications    5    KW 1202

## FEBRUARY

Name_____  Skill: Creative Writing -February

**Choose a sentence and write story about it.**

I made a valentine for ...    A rose is...    I lost my new...

February is...    When I am happy I...    My secret friend...

What time will we...    A pink heart...    The ground will...

Candy hearts...    Can you see...    My ice skates are...

A snowball just...    Look at this! ...    My room is...    I sent...

The mailman...    One day a...

FEBRUARY

*Candy Hearts*

Candy hearts are my favorite Valentines treat. I like to read the messages on them. I like to give them to my friends. Most of all, I like to eat them.

(answers will vary)

© 1996 Kelley Wingate Publications    6    KW 1202

## MARCH

Name_____  Skill: Creative Writing -March

**Choose a sentence and write story about it.**

Now is the time to ...    March is...    Robins and squirrels...

Kites are flying...    We pick teams...    The pot of gold...

I ride my bike to...    Wear green...    Little birds try...

Do you want...    Can I have...

MARCH

*Kites*

Kites are flying in the sky. The wind takes them high above the trees. The bright colors look pretty in the blue sky. Flying kites is a lot of fun.

(answers will vary)

The strong wind ...    Ice cream is...    Windy days make...

On Tuesday we will...    I really like...    If I could, I would...

© 1996 Kelley Wingate Publications    7    KW 1202

## APRIL

Name_____  Skill: Creative Writing -April

**Choose a sentence and write story about it.**

We will hunt for ...    It is time to plant...    The clouds look...

Butterflies...    The rain is...    These eggs...    Will you go...

APRIL

*Flower Garden*

I my garden, we grow many flowers. There are red roses and blue lilacs. In the spring we have tulips and daffodils. I like to smells those pretty flowers. Mom cuts them and puts them in a vase. Flower gardens are nice.

(answers will vary)

This basket is...    My umbrella...    A rainbow...    Good books...

I am ready to...    Puddles are...    A busy bee...    That bush is...

In my garden...    I saw a rabbit...    Lazy ladybugs...

© 1996 Kelley Wingate Publications    8    KW 1202

Name_____ Skill: Creative Writing -May

**Choose a sentence and write story about it.**

| | | |
|---|---|---|
| Our trip to the zoo ... | A dragonfly... | I learned about... |
| May is a good time... | I tripped over... | Tulips and roses... |
| Buds are... | Yesterday I... | I think I am... |

MAY

Trees
I learned about trees
this year. They grow from
seeds. They have sap
that is like our blood.
They have roots, stems
or trunks, and leaves.
I like trees.
(answers will vary)

| | | |
|---|---|---|
| A cowboy rode... | After the storm... | I get mad when... |
| I found a bag with... | Popcorn... | On the way to school... |

© 1996 Kelley Wingate Publications  9  KW 1202

Name_____ Skill: Creative Writing -June

**Choose a sentence and write story about it.**

| | | |
|---|---|---|
| I have a treehouse ... | This summer... | Warm sunshine... |
| My desk is... | We went to the park and... | June is... |
| The teacher said... | After school I... | I feel good about... |
| I will run... | What will I... | I eat breakfast... | How can I... |
| The days are... | I think... | This year was... | Did you really... |

JUNE

This Past Year
This year was fun. I
liked my teacher. The
class made many great
projects. We took a
field trip to the
museum. Our class
play was so much
fun. Best of all I
met Ryan this year.
It was my best
year yet!
(answers will vary)

© 1996 Kelley Wingate Publications  10  KW 1202

Name _____ Skill: Forming Sentences

Every sentence has a beginning and an end.

**Match the beginnings and endings to make five sentences.**

Two yellow ducks — shine in the night.
The boys at the zoo — are fun to read.
The moon and stars — swim in the water.
The happy girl — saw many animals.
Good books — smiled at me.

**Write a beginning for each sentence. Use capitals and end with periods.**

1. Playing is fun.
2. I like to play.
3. Dad goes to work.
4. Joe wears a hat.
5. My food is on the table.

(Answers will vary)

© 1996 Kelley Wingate Publications  11  KW 1202

Name _____ Skill: Forming Sentences

Every sentence has a beginning and an end.

**Match the beginnings and endings to make five sentences.**

The brown dog — took a nap.
Dark clouds — grow in the park.
The mother bird — barked at the cat.
Trees and flowers — filled the sky.
The sleepy boy — made a nest.

**Write a beginning for each sentence. Use capitals and end with periods.**

1. John ate his dinner.
2. Dogs have four legs.
3. I can ride my bike.
4. My friends are here.
5. The sky is blue.

(answers will vary)

© 1996 Kelley Wingate Publications  12  KW 1202

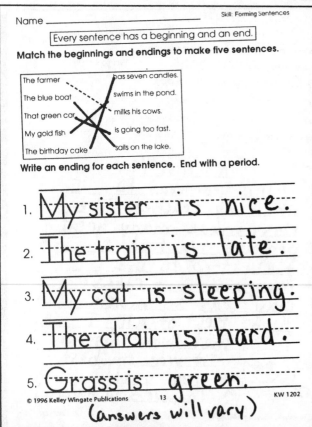

Name _____  Skill: Forming Sentences

Every sentence has a beginning and an end.

**Match the beginnings and endings to make five sentences.**

The farmer — has seven candles.
The blue boat — swims in the pond.
That green car — milks his cows.
My gold fish — is going too fast.
The birthday cake — sails on the lake.

**Write an ending for each sentence. End with a period.**

1. My sister is nice.
2. The train is late.
3. My cat is sleeping.
4. The chair is hard.
5. Grass is green.

© 1996 Kelley Wingate Publications     13     KW 1202

(answers will vary)

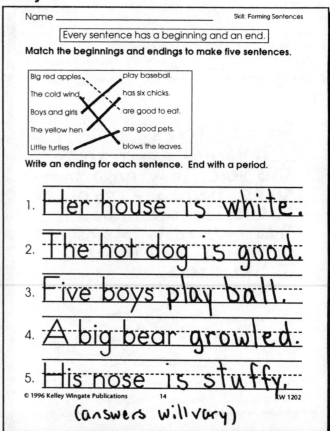

Name _____  Skill: Forming Sentences

Every sentence has a beginning and an end.

**Match the beginnings and endings to make five sentences.**

Big red apples — play baseball.
The cold wind — has six chicks.
Boys and girls — are good to eat.
The yellow hen — are good pets.
Little turtles — blows the leaves.

**Write an ending for each sentence. End with a period.**

1. Her house is white.
2. The hot dog is good.
3. Five boys play ball.
4. A big bear growled.
5. His nose is stuffy.

© 1996 Kelley Wingate Publications     14     KW 1202

(answers will vary)

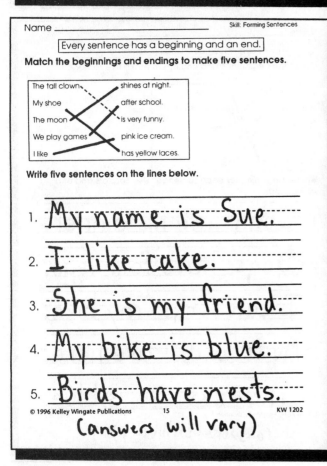

Name _____  Skill: Forming Sentences

Every sentence has a beginning and an end.

**Match the beginnings and endings to make five sentences.**

The tall clown — shines at night.
My shoe — after school.
The moon — is very funny.
We play games — pink ice cream.
I like — has yellow laces.

**Write five sentences on the lines below.**

1. My name is Sue.
2. I like cake.
3. She is my friend.
4. My bike is blue.
5. Birds have nests.

© 1996 Kelley Wingate Publications     15     KW 1202

(answers will vary)

Name _____  Skill: Capitals and Periods

A sentence tells a whole idea.

**Write a sentence about each picture.**
**Begin with a capital and end with a period.**

shoe — This is my brown shoe.

soap — I wash with soap.

dog — The perky dog wagged his tail.

girl — The girl is smiling.

key — This is the key to my house.

© 1996 Kelley Wingate Publications     16     KW 1202

(answers will vary)

# Answer Key

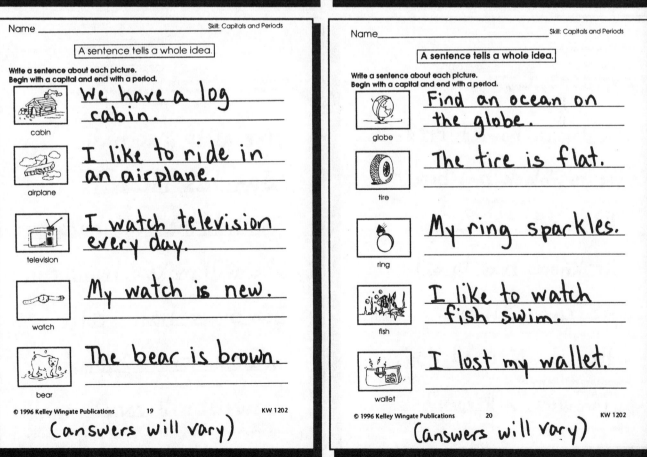

**Name**_____    Skill: Capitals and Periods

A sentence tells a whole idea.

Write a sentence about each picture.
Begin with a capital and end with a period.

train — That is an old train.

strawberry — I love strawberry jam.

umbrella — My umbrella kept me dry.

vase — Put the flowers in a vase.

walrus — The walrus is very big.

© 1996 Kelley Wingate Publications    17    KW 1202

(answers will vary)

**Name**_____    Skill: Capitals and Periods

A sentence tells a whole idea.

Write a sentence about each picture.
Begin with a capital and end with a period.

bike — My bike is green.

mop — Mother will mop the floor.

mouse — This mouse likes cheese.

pig — The pig is fat.

sun — I like to play in the sun.

© 1996 Kelley Wingate Publications    18    KW 1202

(answers will vary)

**Name** _____    Skill: Capitals and Periods

A sentence tells a whole idea.

Write a sentence about each picture.
Begin with a capital and end with a period.

cabin — We have a log cabin.

airplane — I like to ride in an airplane.

television — I watch television every day.

watch — My watch is new.

bear — The bear is brown.

© 1996 Kelley Wingate Publications    19    KW 1202

(answers will vary)

**Name**_____    Skill: Capitals and Periods

A sentence tells a whole idea.

Write a sentence about each picture.
Begin with a capital and end with a period.

globe — Find an ocean on the globe.

tire — The tire is flat.

ring — My ring sparkles.

fish — I like to watch fish swim.

wallet — I lost my wallet.

© 1996 Kelley Wingate Publications    20    KW 1202

(answers will vary)

# Answer Key

Name_____ Skill: Jumbled Sentences

Sentences have order

Unscramble the words to make a sentence.
Write the sentence on the line below it.(Put a period at the end.)

over Summer is

1. Summer is over.

in are back We school

2. We are back in school.

happy to are here be We

3. We are happy to be here.

will read good We books

4. We will read good books.

stories write funny will We

5. We will write funny stories.

all school love We

6. We all love school.

Write your own sentence about school.

7. (answers will vary)

© 1996 Kelley Wingate Publications 21 KW 1202

---

Name_____ Skill: Jumbled Sentences

Sentences have order

Unscramble the words to make a sentence.
Write the sentence on the line below it.(Put a period at the end.)

red had a Bob balloon

1. Bob had a red balloon.

got The away balloon

2. The balloon got away.

after ran He it

3. He ran after it.

him came to Tom help

4. Tom came to help him.

tried both catch it They

5. They both tried to catch it.

it They now have

6. They have it now.

Write your own sentence about a balloon.

7. (answers will vary)

© 1996 Kelley Wingate Publications 22 KW 1202

---

Name_____ Skill: Jumbled Sentences

Sentences have order

Unscramble the words to make a sentence.
Write the sentence on the line below it.(Put a period at the end.)

named dog My is Fred

1. My dog is named Fred.

brown is black He and

2. He is black and brown.

can He tricks do

3. He can do tricks.

to sit knows He how

4. He knows how to sit.

over can roll He

5. He can roll over.

good He dog is

6. He is a good dog.

Write your own sentence your pet.

7. (answers will vary)

© 1996 Kelley Wingate Publications 23 KW 1202

---

Name_____ Skill: Jumbled Sentences

Sentences have order

Unscramble the words to make a sentence.
Write the sentence on the line below it.(Put a period at the end.)

girls ball The play

1. The girls play ball.

has Jan bat the

2. Jan has the bat.

ball The she hard hit

3. She hit the ball hard.

run make She home a will

4. She will make a home run.

ball plays Jan well

5. Jan plays ball well.

all school love We

6. We all love school.

Write your own sentence about baseball.

7. (answers will vary)

© 1996 Kelley Wingate Publications 24 KW 1202

© 1996 Kelley Wingate Publications
CD-3717

# Answer Key

## Page 25

Sentences have order

Unscramble the words to make a sentence.
Write the sentence on the line below it.(Put a period at the end.)

in hops bunny A grass the

1. A bunny hops in the grass.

long two has ears He

2. He has two long ears.

a has He tail white

3. He has a white tail.

nose His wiggles

4. His nose wiggles.

likes eat to He carrots

5. He likes to eat carrots.

home him I take will

6. I will take him home.

Write your own sentence about a bunny.

7. (answers will vary)

© 1996 Kelley Wingate Publications          25          KW 1202

## Page 26

An asking sentence is called a question.  A question ends with a question mark (?).  Words like who, what, where, and when begin questions.

Write a question about each picture.
Begin with a capital and end with a question mark.

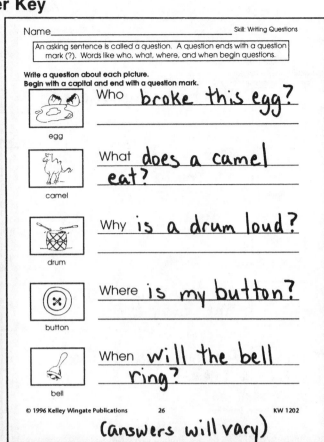

Who broke this egg?
egg

What does a camel eat?
camel

Why is a drum loud?
drum

Where is my button?
button

When will the bell ring?
bell

© 1996 Kelley Wingate Publications          26          KW 1202

(answers will vary)

## Page 27

An asking sentence is called a question.  A question ends with a question mark (?).  Words like who, what, where, and when begin questions.

Write a question about each picture.
Begin with a capital and end with a question mark.

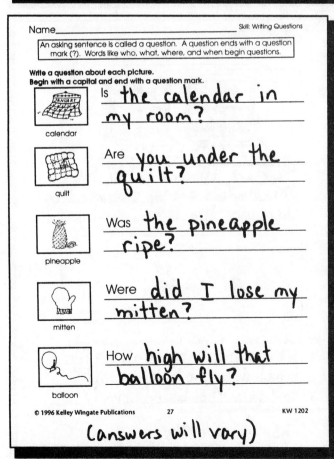

Is the calendar in my room?
calendar

Are you under the quilt?
quilt

Was the pineapple ripe?
pineapple

Were did I lose my mitten?
mitten

How high will that balloon fly?
balloon

© 1996 Kelley Wingate Publications          27          KW 1202

(answers will vary)

## Page 28

An asking sentence is called a question.  A question ends with a question mark (?).  Words like who, what, where, and when begin questions.

Write a question about each picture.
Begin with a capital and end with a question mark.

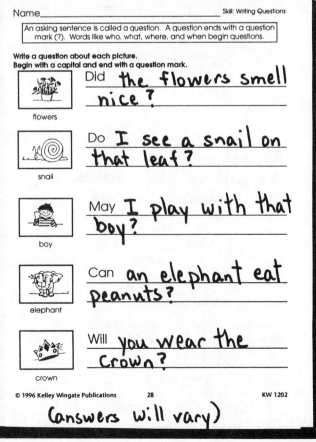

Did the flowers smell nice?
flowers

Do I see a snail on that leaf?
snail

May I play with that boy?
boy

Can an elephant eat peanuts?
elephant

Will you wear the crown?
crown

© 1996 Kelley Wingate Publications          28          KW 1202

(answers will vary)

# Answer Key

Name_____  Skill: Writing Questions

An asking sentence is called a question. A question ends with a question mark (?). Words like who, what, where, and when begin questions.

Write a question about each picture.
Begin with a capital and end with a question mark.

Who **has my skates?**

skates

What **kind of cloud is that?**

cloud

Is **that my basket?**

basket

Are **the knights in the castle?**

castle

Did **you plant that tree?**

tree

© 1996 Kelley Wingate Publications    29    KW 1202

(answers will vary)

---

Name_____  Skill: Writing Questions

An asking sentence is called a question. A question ends with a question mark (?). Words like who, what, where, and when begin questions.

Write a question about each picture.
Begin with a capital and end with a question mark.

Where **is the cow?**

cow

When **did the frog swim away?**

frog

Was **the ladder very tall?**

ladder

Do **you like my new jacket?**

jacket

Can **a goat eat everything?**

goat

© 1996 Kelley Wingate Publications    30    KW 1202

(answers will vary)

---

Name_____  Skill: Writing Statements and questions

Telling sentences are called statements.
Asking sentences are called questions.

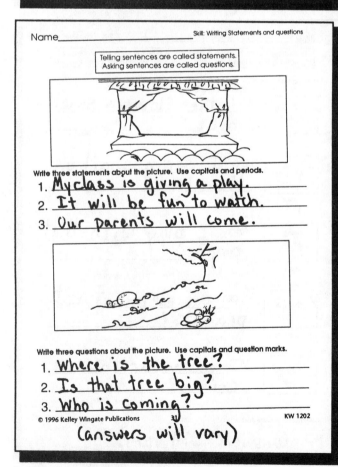

Write three statements about the picture. Use capitals and periods.
1. My class is giving a play.
2. It will be fun to watch.
3. Our parents will come.

Write three questions about the picture. Use capitals and question marks.
1. Where is the tree?
2. Is that tree big?
3. Who is coming?

© 1996 Kelley Wingate Publications    31    KW 1202

(answers will vary)

---

Name_____  Skill: Writing Statements and questions

Telling sentences are called statements.
Asking sentences are called questions.

Write three statements about the picture. Use capitals and periods.
1. There are flowers on the table.
2. The flowers are by the window.
3. There are two large windows.

Write three questions about the picture. Use capitals and question marks.
1. Why is the baby smiling?
2. What does the baby want?
3. How does the baby crawl?

© 1996 Kelley Wingate Publications    32    KW 1202

(answers will vary)

---

© 1996 Kelley Wingate Publications    114    CD-3717

# Answer Key

---

Name_____    Skill: Writing Statements and questions

> Telling sentences are called statements.
> Asking sentences are called questions.

Write three statements about the picture. Use capitals and periods.

1. Alice and Jim are singing.
2. They love to sing.
3. They are singing in a show.

Write three questions about the picture. Use capitals and question marks.

1. Who is behind the tree?
2. Why is she hiding?
3. Is she playing a trick?

© 1996 Kelley Wingate Publications    33    KW 1202

(answers will vary)

---

Name_____    Skill: Writing Statements and questions

> Telling sentences are called statements.
> Asking sentences are called questions.

Write three statements about the picture. Use capitals and periods.

The flowers are growing.
The worm is crawling.
It is a very nice day.

Write three questions about the picture. Use capitals and question marks.

Who made this snowman?
Where is his scarf?
How many buttons does he have?

© 1996 Kelley Wingate Publications    34    KW 1202

(answers will vary)

---

Name_____    Skill: Writing Statements and questions

> Telling sentences are called statements.
> Asking sentences are called questions.

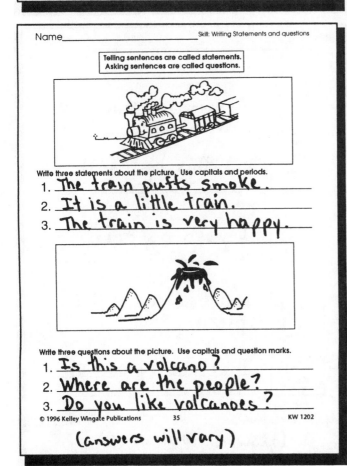

Write three statements about the picture. Use capitals and periods.

1. The train puffs smoke.
2. It is a little train.
3. The train is very happy.

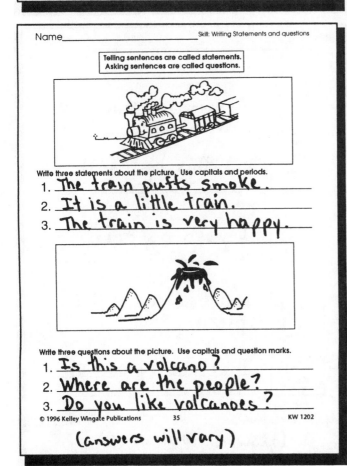

Write three questions about the picture. Use capitals and question marks.

1. Is this a volcano?
2. Where are the people?
3. Do you like volcanoes?

© 1996 Kelley Wingate Publications    35    KW 1202

(answers will vary)

---

Name_____    Skill: Statements and questions

> A statement tells you something and ends with a period.
> A question asks you something and ends with a question mark.

Write a statement or question about each picture.
Begin with a capital. End with a period or question mark.

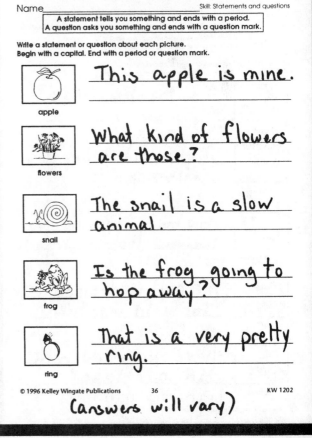

apple — This apple is mine.

flowers — What kind of flowers are those?

snail — The snail is a slow animal.

frog — Is the frog going to hop away?

ring — That is a very pretty ring.

© 1996 Kelley Wingate Publications    36    KW 1202

(answers will vary)

---

# Answer Key

Name_____
Skill: Statements and questions

A statement tells you something and ends with a period.
A question asks you something and ends with a question mark.

Write a statement or question about each picture.
Begin with a capital. End with a period or question mark.

dinosaur
Do you like this dinosaur?

crown
The king wears a crown.

dog
Does the puppy like his bone?

cat
The cat is playing ball.

house
Doesn't that house look warm and cozy?
(Answers will vary)

© 1996 Kelley Wingate Publications      37      KW 1202

---

Name_____
Skill: Statements and questions

A statement tells you something and ends with a period.
A question asks you something and ends with a question mark.

Write a statement or question about each picture.
Begin with a capital. End with a period or question mark.

train
The train is very happy.

tire
Will this tire fit your car?

book
I read a good book yesterday.

tractor
Will the farmer use the tractor today?

globe
A globe is round.
(Answers will vary)

© 1996 Kelley Wingate Publications      38      KW 1202

---

Name_____
Skill: Statements and questions

A statement tells you something and ends with a period.
A question asks you something and ends with a question mark.

Write a statement or question about each picture.
Begin with a capital. End with a period or question mark.

bear
Is the bear cold?

watch
My watch stopped running.

toothbrush
How many times do you use your toothbrush each day?

girl
The girl is dressed for cold weather.

airplane
Have you ridden in an airplane?
(answers will vary)

© 1996 Kelley Wingate Publications      39      KW 1202

---

Name_____
Skill: Statements and questions

A statement tells you something and ends with a period.
A question asks you something and ends with a question mark.

Write a statement or question about each picture.
Begin with a capital. End with a period or question mark.

shoe
My favorite shoes are worn out.

leaf
Did this leaf fall from the tree?

soap
I wash my face with soap.

picture
Did you draw this picture?

box
That pretty box is mine.

© 1996 Kelley Wingate Publications      40      KW 1202

(answers will vary)

---

© 1996 Kelley Wingate Publications      116      CD-3717

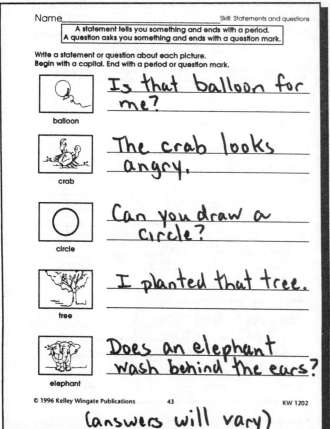

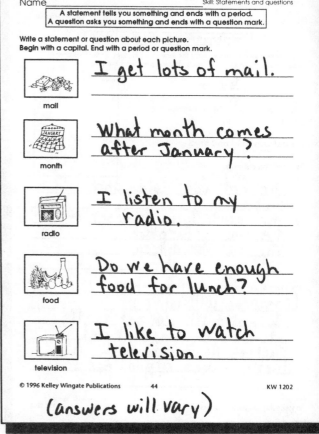

## Panel 1 (page 41)

Name_____  Skill: Statements and questions

A statement tells you something and ends with a period.
A question asks you something and ends with a question mark.

Write a statement or question about each picture.
Begin with a capital. End with a period or question mark.

baby — Is the baby hungry?

swing — I love to swing.

ice cream — Why does ice cream melt?

skates — I hung up my skates.

cloud — Is that a rain cloud? (answers will vary)

© 1996 Kelley Wingate Publications    41    KW 1202

## Panel 2 (page 42)

Name_____  Skill: Statements and questions

A statement tells you something and ends with a period.
A question asks you something and ends with a question mark.

Write a statement or question about each picture.
Begin with a capital. End with a period or question mark.

basket — I put a picnic in the basket.

snake — Does that snake bite?

castle — I wish I were in a castle.

cow — Why is the cow sad?

rabbit — The bunny rabbit is fuzzy.

© 1996 Kelley Wingate Publications    42    KW 1202

## Panel 3 (page 43)

Name_____  Skill: Statements and questions

A statement tells you something and ends with a period.
A question asks you something and ends with a question mark.

Write a statement or question about each picture.
Begin with a capital. End with a period or question mark.

balloon — Is that balloon for me?

crab — The crab looks angry.

circle — Can you draw a circle?

tree — I planted that tree.

elephant — Does an elephant wash behind the ears?

© 1996 Kelley Wingate Publications    43    KW 1202

(answers will vary)

## Panel 4 (page 44)

Name_____  Skill: Statements and questions

A statement tells you something and ends with a period.
A question asks you something and ends with a question mark.

Write a statement or question about each picture.
Begin with a capital. End with a period or question mark.

mail — I get lots of mail.

month — What month comes after January?

radio — I listen to my radio.

food — Do we have enough food for lunch?

television — I like to watch television.

© 1996 Kelley Wingate Publications    44    KW 1202

(answers will vary)

# Answer Key

Name_____

Skill: Statements and questions

> A statement tells you something and ends with a period.
> A question asks you something and ends with a question mark.

Write a statement or question about each picture.
Begin with a capital. End with a period or question mark.

snow — Will it snow all day?

beach — I love to go to the beach.

sun — Is the sun out today?

pig — The pig loves to eat.

pizza — Would you like a slice of pizza?

© 1996 Kelley Wingate Publications    45    KW 1202

(answers will vary)

---

Name_____

Skill: Sequencing

> Stories have a beginning, middle, and end.

These sentences tell a story. Write the sentences in order on the lines below.
Be sure to use capitals and periods. Draw a picture for the story.

**Lost Tooth**

During lunch I bit into an apple.

My tooth got stuck in the apple.

My tooth was wiggly and loose.

1. My tooth was wiggly and loose.
2. During lunch I bit into an apple.
3. My tooth got stuck in the apple.

Have you lost a tooth? Write about it.

I lost my first tooth when I was five. It was the front tooth on the top row. I got a dollar from the Tooth Fairy!

(answers will vary)

© 1996 Kelley Wingate Publications    46    KW 1202

---

Name_____

Skill: Sequencing

> Stories have a beginning, middle, and end.

These sentences tell a story. Write the sentences in order on the lines below.
Be sure to use capitals and periods. Draw a picture for the story.

**The Cat**

She curled up in front of the warm fireplace.

The cat was cold and tired.

The cat fell asleep.

1. The cat was cold and tired.
2. She curled up in front of the warm fireplace.
3. The cat fell asleep.

What kind of pet would you like to have? Write about it.

(Answers will vary.)
I would like a pet turtle. It would be a quiet pet. Turtles don't eat much. A turtle makes a good pet.

© 1996 Kelley Wingate Publications    47    KW 1202

---

Name_____

Skill: Sequencing

> Stories have a beginning, middle, and end.

These sentences tell a story. Write the sentences in order on the lines below.
Be sure to use capitals and periods. Draw a picture for the story.

**A Letter**

I wrote a letter to my best friend.

I put the letter into the mailbox.

I licked the envelope and put on a stamp.

1. I wrote a letter to my best friend.
2. I licked the envelope and put on a stamp.
3. I put the letter into the mailbox.

Have you ever gotten mail? Write about it.

(Answers will vary.)
I got a letter from my pen pal. She lives in Japan. We write to each other.

© 1996 Kelley Wingate Publications    48    KW 1202

---

---

Name _____    Skill: Sequencing

| Stories have a beginning, middle, and end. |

These sentences tell a story. Write the sentences in order on the lines below.
Be sure to use capitals and periods. Draw a picture for the story.

**A New Friend**

The horse was very big and I was scared!

I gave him a carrot and we became friends.

I went horseback riding last week.

1. I went horseback riding last week.
2. The horse was very big and I was scared.
3. I gave him a carrot and we became friends.

Can you ride a horse? Write about it.

(Answers will vary.)
    I ride my cousin's horse. Its name is Brownie. It is very tall. I like to ride Brownie.

© 1996 Kelley Wingate Publications    49    KW 1202

---

Name _____    Skill: Sequencing

| Stories have a beginning, middle, and end. |

These sentences tell a story. Write the sentences in order on the lines below.
Be sure to use capitals and periods. Draw a picture for the story.

**Baby Chick**

There were ten eggs in the warm box.

Out popped a fuzzy baby chick!

Suddenly one egg jiggled and cracked open.

1. There were ten eggs in a warm box.
2. Suddenly one egg jiggled and cracked open.
3. Out popped a fuzzy baby chick.

What would you see on a farm? Write about it.

(Answers will vary.)
    A farm has many animals. There are cows and chickens. There are goats and sheep. I like farm animals.

© 1996 Kelley Wingate Publications    50    KW 1202

---

Name _____    Skill: Story Elements

| Stories tell about someone doing something. |

Pictures can tell a story. Draw a picture of a child who has chicken pox.
Add something of your own to the picture. Answer the questions about your "picture story".

1. Who is this story about? This story is about Roger.
2. Where does this story take place? He is in his bedroom
3. What happens first? He gets the chicken pox.
4. What happens next? His friends send him cards.
5. How does the story end? Roger feels happier.

Have you ever been sick? Write about it.

When I was very young I was very ill. I had a high fever. Mom and Dad were worried. They stayed up all night to watch me. By morning the fever was gone.
(answers will vary)

© 1996 Kelley Wingate Publications    51    KW 1202

---

Name _____    Skill: Story Elements

| Stories tell about someone doing something. |

Pictures can tell a story. Draw a picture of a snowman. Put a funny hat on his head. Add something of your own to the picture. Answer the questions about your "picture story".

1. Who is this story about? This story is about Iceman.
2. Where does this story take place? He is in Sue's back yard.
3. What happens first? Sue and Joe build a snowman.
4. What happens next? They give him eyes, arms, and a hat.
5. How does the story end? They name the snowman Iceman.

What would you do in the snow? Write about it.

I would love to play in the snow. I would make footprints. I would make snowballs for a snowball fight. I like snow.
(answers will vary)

© 1996 Kelley Wingate Publications    52    KW 1202

---

# Answer Key

Name _____

Skill: Story Elements

| Stories tell about someone doing something. |

Pictures can tell a story. Draw a picture of a birdhouse in a tree. Add something of your own to the picture. Answer the questions about your "picture story".

1. Who is this story about? This story is about Mother bird.
2. Where does this story take place? She is in the tree.
3. What happens first? Mother bird sits on her nest.
4. What happens next? She feels the eggs cracking open.
5. How does the story end? Mother bird feeds the babies.

Have you ever watched a bird? Write about it.
I saw a very strange bird. It was just a tiny thing. It was chasing a squirrel. The squirrel was running away as the tiny bird pecked at its tail.
(answers will vary)

© 1996 Kelley Wingate Publications          53          KW 1202

---

Name _____

Skill: Story Elements

| Stories tell about someone doing something. |

Pictures can tell a story. Draw a picture of a present with a big bow. Add something of your own to the picture. Answer the questions about your "picture story".

1. Who is this story about? This story is about a birthday party.
2. Where does this story take place? Jason is having the party at his house.
3. What happens first? Jason sends invitations to all his friends.
4. What happens next? They come to the party.
5. How does the story end? They eat cake and ice cream.

What would you like for a present? Write about it.
I would like a new bike for a present. My bike used to be my brother's. It is rusty and the tires are worn. I would really love a shiny new bike.
(answers will vary)

© 1996 Kelley Wingate Publications          54          KW 1202

---

Name _____

Skill: Story Elements

| Stories tell about someone doing something. |

Pictures can tell a story. Draw a picture of a large orange pumpkin still on the vine. Add something of your own to the picture. Answer the questions about your "picture story".

1. Who is this story about? This picture is about the pumpkin.
2. Where does this story take place? It is in the garden.
3. What happens first? The pumpkin grows large and orange.
4. What happens next? It is happy to be so big.
5. How does the story end? A boy takes the pumpkin home.

Do you have a special plant in your home or yard? Write about it.
I have an oak tree in my yard. I found an oak seedling at the park. I took it home. Dad and I planted it in the back yard. It is almost as tall as me!
(answers will vary)

© 1996 Kelley Wingate Publications          55          KW 1202

---

Name _____

Skill: Story Elements

| Stories tell about someone doing something. |

Pictures can tell a story. Draw a picture of a a magician pulling a rabbit out of a hat. Add something of your own to the picture. Answer the questions about your "picture story".

1. Who is this story about? This story is about a magician.
2. Where does this story take place? The magician is at a birthday party.
3. What happens first? The magician does many tricks.
4. What happens next? He pulls a rabbit from his hat.
5. How does the story end? The rabbit disappears!

Have you ever seen a magic show? Write about it.
Once my uncle took me to a magic show. The magician made a lady float. He sawed a man in half! I liked watching his tricks.
(answers will vary)

© 1996 Kelley Wingate Publications          56          KW 1202

Name _____     Skill: Story Elements

| Stories tell about someone doing something. |

**Pictures can tell a story.** Draw a picture of yourself. Add something of your own to the picture. Answer the questions about your "picture story".

1. Who is this story about? This story is about me.
2. Where does this story take place? I am with my Grandmother.
3. What happens first? I went to spend the night with Grandma.
4. What happens next? We baked cookies and read books.
5. How does the story end? Grandma kissed me good night.

What is special about you? Write about it.

I have a special hobby. I collect buttons. There are 200 buttons in my collection. They are very pretty.

(answers will vary)

© 1996 Kelley Wingate Publications    57      KW 1202

---

Name _____     Skill: Story Elements

| Stories tell about someone doing something. |

**Pictures can tell a story.** Draw a picture of your favorite flowers. Add something of your own to the picture. Answer the questions about your "picture story".

1. Who is this story about? This story is about roses.
2. Where does this story take place? The roses are on the table.
3. What happens first? I cut some roses from the bush.
4. What happens next? I took off the thorns and put the roses in a vase.
5. How does the story end? I gave the flowers to my mother.

What are your favorite kind of flowers? Write about them.

My favorite flowers are roses. I like yellow roses best. Yellow roses smell so nice. We grow them in my garden. I will have yellow rose bushes when I grow up.

(answers will vary)

© 1996 Kelley Wingate Publications    58      KW 1202

---

Name _____     Skill: Story Elements

| Stories tell about someone doing something. |

**Pictures can tell a story.** Draw a picture of a pair of shoes. Show the laces in bows. Add something of your own to the picture. Answer the questions about your "picture story".

1. Who is this story about? This story is about Kesha's shoes.
2. Where does this story take place? The shoes are under Kesha's bed.
3. What happens first? Kesha was looking for her shoes.
4. What happens next? She looks everywhere for them.
5. How does the story end? Kesha finds her shoes under the bed.

Can you tie your shoes? Write about it.

I can tie my shoes. I learned when I was five years old. My big brother, Raymond, showed me how to do it. I practiced and practiced. I was proud when I learned how.

(answers will vary)

© 1996 Kelley Wingate Publications    59      KW 1202

---

Name _____     Skill: Story Elements

| Stories tell about someone doing something. |

**Pictures can tell a story.** Draw a picture of a scary Halloween costume. Add something of your own to the picture. Answer the questions about your "picture story".

1. Who is this story about? This story is about Joe scaring Frank.
2. Where does this story take place? The boys are at Joe's house.
3. What happens first? Joe puts on the scary costume.
4. What happens next? Joe jumps out of the closet when Frank comes in.
5. How does the story end? Frank is scared.

What were you dressed as last Halloween? Write about it.

I dressed as a ghost last Halloween. I cut two eye holes in a sheet. I wore the sheet trick-or-treating. I couldn't eat the candy because there was no mouth hole!

(answers will vary)

© 1996 Kelley Wingate Publications    60      KW 1202

## Whale Watching

Name _____ Skill: Word Box Story

Stories have a beginning, a middle, and an end.

**Word Box**

whale
huge
water
blow
air
tail
grey
fins

### Whale Watching

A huge whale was swimming one day. She was blowing water high into the air. Her strong tail pushed her quickly through the water. I could see her grey fins when she rolled over. The whale was fun to watch.
(answers will vary)

**Things to think about:**
Who is this story about? Where does the story take place? How does this story begin? What happens next? How does the story end?

© 1996 Kelley Wingate Publications          61          KW 1202

---

Name _____ Skill: Word Box Story

Stories have a beginning, a middle, and an end.

**Word Box**

camping
woods
tent
cook
flashlight
fire
sleep
bugs

### The Camping Trip

Mack went camping in the woods. He set up his tent and made a small fire. He began to cook his dinner but bugs were biting him. Mack decided to read but it was too dark. He used his flashlight for awhile, but fell asleep.
(answers will vary)

**Things to think about:**
Who is this story about? Where does the story take place? How does this story begin? What happens next? How does the story end?

© 1996 Kelley Wingate Publications          62          KW 1202

---

Name _____ Skill: Word Box Story

Stories have a beginning, a middle, and an end.

Use the words in the word box to write a story about the picture. Remember to use capitals and periods. Make a title for your story.

**Word Box**

skis
mittens
boots
snow
hills
fun
ice
winter

### Skiing

Skiing is a great sport. You must wear mittens, boots, and a warm coat. The skis glide over the soft snow. It is best to start on small hills. Watch out for patches of ice! The best winter sport is skiing.
(answers will vary)

**Things to think about:**
Who is this story about? Where does the story take place? How does this story begin? What happens next? How does the story end?

© 1996 Kelley Wingate Publications          63          KW 1202

---

Name _____ Skill: Word Box Story

Stories have a beginning, a middle, and an end.

Use the words in the word box to write a story about the picture. Remember to use capitals and periods. Make a title for your story.

**Word Box**

people
afraid
pray
sing
dance
clap
alone
stage

### Stage Fright

Brian was in a play. Many people came to see it. Brian had to sing and dance on stage. He was suddenly afraid to go on stage. He would be all alone out there. He took a deep breath, prayed and went on. The audience clapped.
(answers will vary)

**Things to think about:**
Who is this story about? Where does the story take place? How does this story begin? What happens next? How does the story end?

© 1996 Kelley Wingate Publications          64          KW 1202

# Answer Key

Name _____   Skill: Word Box Story

Stories have a beginning, a middle, and an end.

Use the words in the word box to write a story about the picture.
Remember to use capitals and periods. Make a title for your story.

**Word Box**

pool
swim
splash
float
water
diving
towel
jump

## Pool Time

We have a pool in my yard. My
friends and I love to swim and
splash each other. We have diving
contests or see who can float the
longest. We jump in the deep end.
After that we dry off on a towel
and relax in the sun.

(answers will vary)

**Things to think about:**
Who is this story about? Where does the story take place? How does this story begin?
What happens next? How does the story end?

© 1996 Kelley Wingate Publications        65        KW 1202

---

Name _____   Skill: Word Box Story

Stories have a beginning, a middle, and an end.

Use the words in the word box to write a story about the picture.
Remember to use capitals and periods. Make a title for your story.

**Word Box**

duck
swim
water
splash
feathers
quack
friends
fun

## Pond Fun

One day a duck with green
feathers was swimming on the
pond. It quacked and splashed
water everywhere. Soon some
of the ducks friends came to
join him. They had a lot of
fun.

(answers will vary)

**Things to think about:**
Who is this story about? Where does the story take place? How does this story begin?
What happens next? How does the story end?

© 1996 Kelley Wingate Publications        66        KW 1202

---

Name _____   Skill: Word Box Story

Stories have a beginning, a middle, and an end.

Use the words in the word box to write a story about the picture.
Remember to use capitals and periods. Make a title for your story.

**Word Box**

worm
crawl
flowers
happy
slowly
grass
leaves
green

## Lunch

A little worm crawled across
the grass. He saw some pretty
flowers and wanted to eat the
green leaves. The worm crawled
slowly to those flowers. He ate
three leaves and was happy.

(answers will vary)

**Things to think about:**
Who is this story about? Where does the story take place? How does this story begin?
What happens next? How does the story end?

© 1996 Kelley Wingate Publications        67        KW 1202

---

Name _____   Skill: Word Box Story

Stories have a beginning, a middle, and an end.

Use the words in the word box to write a story about the picture.
Remember to use capitals and periods. Make a title for your story.

**Word Box**

kangaroo
tail
pouch
strong
jump
legs
baby
hop

## Matilda

Matilda is a mother kangaroo.
She keeps her baby in a pouch.
When danger is near, she uses
her strong legs and tail to
hop quickly away. Someday her
baby will learn to jump, too.

(answers will vary)

**Things to think about:**
Who is this story about? Where does the story take place? How does this story begin?
What happens next? How does the story end?

© 1996 Kelley Wingate Publications        68        KW 1202

---

# Answer Key

---

Name _____  Skill: Word Box Story

Stories have a beginning, a middle, and an end.

Use the words in the word box to write a story about the picture.
Remember to use capitals and periods. Make a title for your story.

**Word Box**

house
bird
fly
tree
food
seed
far
wings

## House Hunting

Robin was a little bird who needed
a house. Each day she would fly
far and wide looking for one.
She always saw seeds and other
food, but no house. Her wings
grew tired, but she didn't stop. One
day she saw a house in a tree. It
was her new home. (answers will vary)

**Things to think about:**
Who is this story about? Where does the story take place? How does this story begin?
What happens next? How does the story end?

© 1996 Kelley Wingate Publications       69       KW 1202

---

Name _____  Skill: Word Box Story

Stories have a beginning, a middle, and an end.

Use the words in the word box to write a story about the picture.
Remember to use capitals and periods. Make a title for your story.

**Word Box**

ocean
waves
water
octopus
eight
deep
legs
wet

## The Octopus

The octopus lives deep in the
ocean. It has eight long legs.
It stays wet in the water.
Sometimes it plays in the
waves. The octopus is an
interesting animal.

(answers will vary)

**Things to think about:**
Who is this story about? Where does the story take place? How does this story begin?
What happens next? How does the story end?

© 1996 Kelley Wingate Publications       70       KW 1202

---

Name _____  Skill: Word Box Story

Stories have a beginning, a middle, and an end.

Add 5 more words to the word box and use them to write a story about the
picture. Remember to use capitals and periods. Make a title for your story.

**Word Box**
frog
pond
leap
lily
fly
eat
splash
hop

## Silly Frog

A frog was sitting on a lily pad.
He was hungry. A fly came by.
The frog leaped and hopped. He
tried to catch that fly. Splash!
He landed in the pond. The fly
got away.

(answers will vary)

**Things to think about:**
Who is this story about? Where does the story take place? How does this story
begin? What happens next? How does the story end?

© 1996 Kelley Wingate Publications       71       KW 1202

---

Name _____  Skill: Word Box Story

Stories have a beginning, a middle, and an end.

Add 5 more words to the word box and use them to write a story about the
picture. Remember to use capitals and periods. Make a title for your story.

**Word Box**
ladder
tree
apples
tasty
red
juicy
knee
fell

## Apple Picking

I wanted an apple from my tree.
I got a ladder and climbed to a
high branch. I picked a juicy
red apple and took a big bite.
It was tasty. It was so good I
forgot to hold on. I fell and hurt
my knee.

(answers will vary)

**Things to think about:**
Who is this story about? Where does the story take place? How does this story
begin? What happens next? How does the story end?

© 1996 Kelley Wingate Publications       72       KW 1202

---

# Answer Key

Name_____   Skill: Word Box Story

Stories have a beginning, a middle, and an end.

Add 5 more words to the word box and use them to write a story about the picture. Remember to use capitals and periods. Make a title for your story.

Word Box
chair
fell
book
read
lean
help
tipped
grab

## Help!

I was sitting in a chair reading a good book. I leaned back and the chair began to tip. It tipped further and I fell over backward. I tried to grab the table but I missed. Mother came to help. She said never to lean on the chair again.
(answers will vary)

**Things to think about:**
Who is this story about? Where does the story take place? How does this story begin? What happens next? How does the story end?

© 1996 Kelley Wingate Publications          73          KW 1202

---

Name_____   Skill: Word Box Story

Stories have a beginning, a middle, and an end

Add 5 more words to the word box and use them to write a story about the picture. Remember to use capitals and periods. Make a title for your story.

Word Box
giraffe
neck
leaves
long
bend
reach
eat
water

## Too Long

The giraffe has a long neck. That is so it can reach leaves high in trees. The long neck cannot reach the ground. The giraffe must bend its knees so it can get a drink of water. I am glad my neck is not so long.
(answers will vary)

**Things to think about:**
Who is this story about? Where does the story take place? How does this story begin? What happens next? How does the story end?

© 1996 Kelley Wingate Publications          74          KW 1202

---

Name_____   Skill: Word Box Story

Stories have a beginning, a middle, and an end.

Add 5 more words to the word box and use them to write a story about the picture. Remember to use capitals and periods. Make a title for your story.

Word Box
skates
wheels
roll
practice
fast
race
sparks
good

## Skating

I love to skate. I practice every day. I race down the sidewalk as fast as I can. My wheels spin until sparks fly! I am a very good skater, but my skates are wearing out. I will need some new ones soon.
(answers will vary)

**Things to think about:**
Who is this story about? Where does the story take place? How does this story begin? What happens next? How does the story end?

© 1996 Kelley Wingate Publications          75          KW 1202

---

Name_____   Skill: Word Box Story

Stories have a beginning, a middle, and an end.

Add 5 more words to the word box and use them to write a story about the picture. Remember to use capitals and periods. Make a title for your story.

Word Box
parrot
perch
cracker
feathers
green
blue
sharp
beak

## Strange Bird

Mr. Todd has a pretty parrot. Her feathers are green, blue and yellow. She has a large beak that is very sharp. The parrot sits on a perch and asks for carrots. I though parrots liked crackers.
(answers will vary)

**Things to think about:**
Who is this story about? Where does the story take place? How does this story begin? What happens next? How does the story end?

© 1996 Kelley Wingate Publications          76          KW 1202

---

## Worksheet 1 (page 77)

Name_____

Skill: Word Box Story

Stories have a beginning, a middle, and an end.

Add 5 more words to the word box and use them to write a story about the picture. Remember to use capitals and periods. Make a title for your story.

**Word Box**
giant
friend
frighten
children
smile
tree
hand
help

### The Friendly Giant

Meg was a giant. Children were frightened of her because she was so big. One day David got stuck in a tree. The children didn't know what to do. Meg smiled. She reached out and took David in her hand. She put him down. The children were happy. Meg was their friend.
(answers will vary)

**Things to think about:**
Who is this story about? Where does the story take place? How does this story begin? What happens next? How does the story end?

## Worksheet 2 (page 78)

Name_____

Skill: Word Box Story

Stories have a beginning, a middle, and an end.

Add 5 more words to the word box and use them to write a story about the picture. Remember to use capitals and periods. Make a title for your story.

**Word Box**
sleepy
girl
dream
pillow
chase
run
woke
scared

### A Silly Dream

A little girl was sleepy. She took a nap. She dreamed that a huge pillow was chasing her. She began to run. The pillow kept coming. Suddenly the girl woke up. Her pillow was over her head. She knew it was silly to be scared of a pillow.
(answers will vary)

**Things to think about:**
Who is this story about? Where does the story take place? How does this story begin? What happens next? How does the story end?

## Worksheet 3 (page 79)

Name_____

Skill: Word Box Story

Stories have a beginning, a middle, and an end.

Add 5 more words to the word box and use them to write a story about the picture. Remember to use capitals and periods. Make a title for your story.

**Word Box**
castle
bridge
moat
golden
hill
princess
tower
save

### The Castle

Once there was a golden castle. It sat on top of a hill. A moat went around the castle. A princess was in the highest tower. A prince came to save her. He lowered the bridge and crossed the moat. They married and lived happily ever after.
(answers will vary)

**Things to think about:**
Who is this story about? Where does the story take place? How does this story begin? What happens next? How does the story end?

## Worksheet 4 (page 80)

Name_____

Skill: Word Box Story

Stories have a beginning, a middle, and an end.

Add 5 more words to the word box and use them to write a story about the picture. Remember to use capitals and periods. Make a title for your story.

**Word Box**
owl
night
wise
house
fence
fly
walk
hoot

### Wise Owl

An old owl used to live near my house. Every night he would fly to my fence and sit there. He had big eyes. I could walk right up to him and he wouldn't fly away. He would hoot at me, though. He was a wise old owl.
(answers will vary)

**Things to think about:**
Who is this story about? Where does the story take place? How does this story begin? What happens next? How does the story end?

# Answer Key

Name _____    Skill: Word Box Story

Stories have a beginning, a middle, and an end.

Use the words in the story web to write a story about the picture.
Remember to use capitals and periods. Make a title for your story.

flutter   wings

butterfly

yellow   flowers

### Butterflies

Butterflies are beautiful insects. They flutter and flit on the wind. Their wings look too fragile to fly! They like the yellow flowers in my yard. I like to watch them come and go.

(answers will vary)

**Things to think about:**
Who is this story about? Where does the story take place? How does this story begin? What happens next? How does the story end?

© 1996 Kelley Wingate Publications    81    KW 1202

---

Name _____    Skill: Word Box Story

Stories have a beginning, a middle, and an end.

Use the words in the story web to write a story about the picture.
Remember to use capitals and periods. Make a title for your story.

stores   bus

city

cars   people

BANK
MARKET

### My City

I live in a city. There are many stores to shop in. There are also a lot of cars and people. Many people take the bus to work. The city is a busy place.

(answers will vary)

**Things to think about:**
Who is this story about? Where does the story take place? How does this story begin? What happens next? How does the story end?

© 1996 Kelley Wingate Publications    82    KW 1202

---

Name _____    Skill: Word Box Story

Stories have a beginning, a middle, and an end.

Use the words in the story web to write a story about the picture.
Remember to use capitals and periods. Make a title for your story.

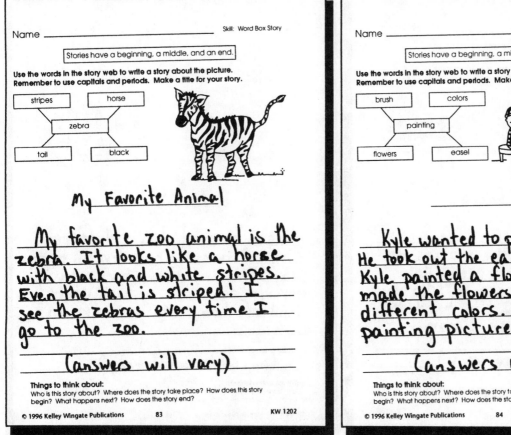

stripes   horse

zebra

tail   black

### My Favorite Animal

My favorite zoo animal is the zebra. It looks like a horse with black and white stripes. Even the tail is striped! I see the zebras every time I go to the zoo.

(answers will vary)

**Things to think about:**
Who is this story about? Where does the story take place? How does this story begin? What happens next? How does the story end?

© 1996 Kelley Wingate Publications    83    KW 1202

---

Name _____    Skill: Word Box Story

Stories have a beginning, a middle, and an end.

Use the words in the story web to write a story about the picture.
Remember to use capitals and periods. Make a title for your story.

brush   colors

painting

flowers   easel

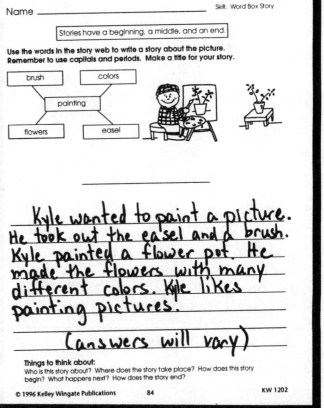

Kyle wanted to paint a picture. He took out the easel and a brush. Kyle painted a flower pot. He made the flowers with many different colors. Kyle likes painting pictures.

(answers will vary)

**Things to think about:**
Who is this story about? Where does the story take place? How does this story begin? What happens next? How does the story end?

© 1996 Kelley Wingate Publications    84    KW 1202

# Answer Key

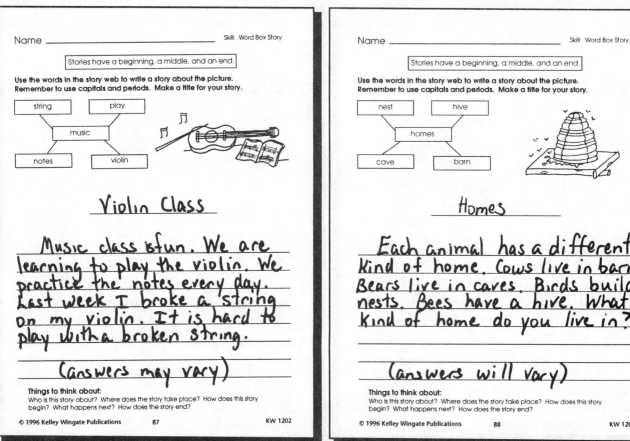

---

Name _____    Skill: Word Box Story

| Stories have a beginning, a middle, and an end. |

Use the words in the story web to write a story about the picture.
Remember to use capitals and periods. Make a title for your story.

tail    wind
kite
string    clouds

## My Kite

One windy day I went kite
flying. I tied a string to my
orange kite and let the wind take
it up. My kite raced the clouds.
Its tail was waving behind it.
I love to fly my kite.

(answers will vary)

**Things to think about:**
Who is this story about? Where does the story take place? How does this story
begin? What happens next? How does the story end?

© 1996 Kelley Wingate Publications        85        KW 1202

---

Name _____    Skill: Word Box Story

| Stories have a beginning, a middle, and an end. |

Use the words in the story web to write a story about the picture.
Remember to use capitals and periods. Make a title for your story.

hiss    long
snake
bite    slide

## Close Call

Cowboy Andy was walking in
the mountains. Suddenly he
heard a hiss by his feet. A long
snake was near the path. Andy
stood still. He was afraid the
snake would bite him. The snake
turned and began to slide away. It was
afraid of Andy!  (answers will vary)

**Things to think about:**
Who is this story about? Where does the story take place? How does this story
begin? What happens next? How does the story end?

© 1996 Kelley Wingate Publications        86        KW 1202

---

Name _____    Skill: Word Box Story

| Stories have a beginning, a middle, and an end. |

Use the words in the story web to write a story about the picture.
Remember to use capitals and periods. Make a title for your story.

string    play
music
notes    violin

## Violin Class

Music class is fun. We are
learning to play the violin. We
practice the notes every day.
Last week I broke a string
on my violin. It is hard to
play with a broken string.

(answers may vary)

**Things to think about:**
Who is this story about? Where does the story take place? How does this story
begin? What happens next? How does the story end?

© 1996 Kelley Wingate Publications        87        KW 1202

---

Name _____    Skill: Word Box Story

| Stories have a beginning, a middle, and an end. |

Use the words in the story web to write a story about the picture.
Remember to use capitals and periods. Make a title for your story.

nest    hive
homes
cave    barn

## Homes

Each animal has a different
kind of home. Cows live in barns.
Bears live in caves. Birds build
nests. Bees have a hive. What
kind of home do you live in?

(answers will vary)

**Things to think about:**
Who is this story about? Where does the story take place? How does this story
begin? What happens next? How does the story end?

© 1996 Kelley Wingate Publications        88        KW 1202

---

# Answer Key

## [Top Left]

Name _____  Skill: Word Box Story

Stories have a beginning, a middle, and an end.

Use the words in the story web to write a story about the picture.
Remember to use capitals and periods. Make a title for your story.

sun — colors
rainbow
rain — clouds

### After the Storm.

We had a big storm yesterday.
It rained a lot. Soon the rain
stopped. The clouds moved away. The
sun began to shine and a rainbow
filled the sky. The rainbow had every
color you can think of. What a nice
ending to a storm.
(answers will vary)

**Things to think about:**
Who is this story about? Where does the story take place? How does this story
begin? What happens next? How does the story end?

© 1996 Kelley Wingate Publications          89          KW 1202

## [Top Right]

Name _____  Skill: Word Box Story

Stories have a beginning, a middle, and an end.

Use the words in the story web to write a story about the picture.
Remember to use capitals and periods. Make a title for your story.

rings — fur
raccoon
mask — paws

### Night Visitor

We were camping. I heard
a noise coming from our ice
chest. I shined the flashlight on it
and saw a raccoon. The raccoon
had a mask around its eyes and
rings on its tail. It had fur everywhere
but its paws. What a cute animal.
(answers will vary)

**Things to think about:**
Who is this story about? Where does the story take place? How does this story
begin? What happens next? How does the story end?

© 1996 Kelley Wingate Publications          90          KW 1202

## [Bottom Left]

Name _____  Skill: Word Box Story

Stories have a beginning, a middle, and an end.

Finish the story web then use the words to write a story about the picture.
Remember to use capitals and periods. Make a title for your story.

teacher — friends
school
bookbag — fun

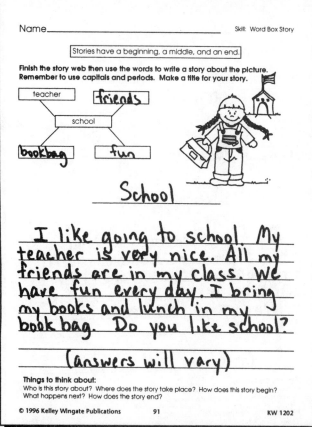

### School

I like going to school. My
teacher is very nice. All my
friends are in my class. We
have fun every day. I bring
my books and lunch in my
book bag. Do you like school?

(answers will vary)

**Things to think about:**
Who is this story about? Where does the story take place? How does this story begin?
What happens next? How does the story end?

© 1996 Kelley Wingate Publications          91          KW 1202

## [Bottom Right]

Name _____  Skill: Word Box Story

Stories have a beginning, a middle, and an end.

Finish the story web then use the words to write a story about the picture.
Remember to use capitals and periods. Make a title for your story.

bunny — carrots
spring
garden — hopped

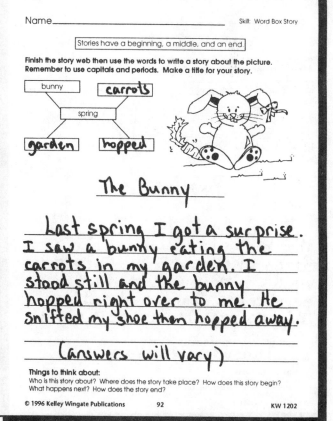

### The Bunny

Last spring I got a surprise.
I saw a bunny eating the
carrots in my garden. I
stood still and the bunny
hopped right over to me. He
sniffed my shoe then hopped away.

(answers will vary)

**Things to think about:**
Who is this story about? Where does the story take place? How does this story begin?
What happens next? How does the story end?

© 1996 Kelley Wingate Publications          92          KW 1202

## Page 93

Name_____  Skill: Word Box Story

Stories have a beginning, a middle, and an end.

Finish the story web then use the words to write a story about the picture.
Remember to use capitals and periods. Make a title for your story.

tent    elephant
circus
clowns    laugh

### The Circus

A circus came to town. Up
went the big tent. In went
the elephants. Clowns ran around
making people laugh. Many
people watched the show. Everyone
had a good time.

(answers will vary)

**Things to think about:**
Who is this story about? Where does the story take place? How does this story begin?
What happens next? How does the story end?

© 1996 Kelley Wingate Publications    93    KW 1202

## Page 94

Name_____  Skill: Word Box Story

Stories have a beginning, a middle, and an end.

Finish the story web then use the words to write a story about the picture.
Remember to use capitals and periods. Make a title for your story.

outside    children
summer
sunshine    swim

### Summer

Summer is the best time of
year. Children play outside in
the sunshine. Warm rains
make the plants grow. Most
people like to swim in outdoor
pools. Summer is very relaxing.

(answers will vary)

**Things to think about:**
Who is this story about? Where does the story take place? How does this story begin?
What happens next? How does the story end?

© 1996 Kelley Wingate Publications    94    KW 1202

## Page 95

Name_____  Skill: Word Box Story

Stories have a beginning, a middle, and an end.

Finish the story web then use the words to write a story about the picture.
Remember to use capitals and periods. Make a title for your story.

puppy    fetch
pets
walk    best

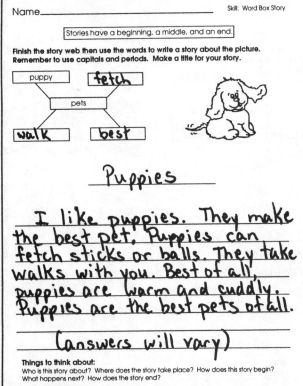

### Puppies

I like puppies. They make
the best pet. Puppies can
fetch sticks or balls. They take
walks with you. Best of all,
puppies are warm and cuddly.
Puppies are the best pets of all.

(answers will vary)

**Things to think about:**
Who is this story about? Where does the story take place? How does this story begin?
What happens next? How does the story end?

© 1996 Kelley Wingate Publications    95    KW 1202

## Page 96

Name_____  Skill: Word Box Story

Stories have a beginning, a middle, and an end.

Finish the story web then use the words to write a story about the picture.
Remember to use capitals and periods. Make a title for your story.

cake    favorite
food
icing    chocolate

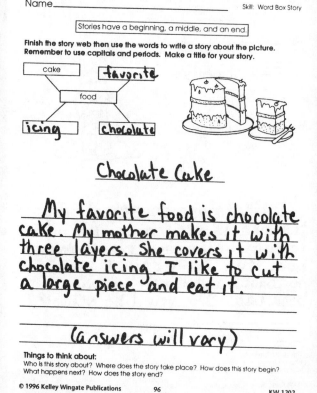

### Chocolate Cake

My favorite food is chocolate
cake. My mother makes it with
three layers. She covers it with
chocolate icing. I like to cut
a large piece and eat it.

(answers will vary)

**Things to think about:**
Who is this story about? Where does the story take place? How does this story begin?
What happens next? How does the story end?

© 1996 Kelley Wingate Publications    96    KW 1202

| | | | |
|---|---|---|---|
| away | April | animal | always |
| bike | bed | bear | basket |
| carrot | brown | both | blow |
| circus | children | chair | catch |

| | | | |
|---|---|---|---|
| dinner | egg | feet | four |
| December | eat | February | firemen |
| cloud | dollar | fairy | fire |
| clock | dinosaur | elephant | fence |

| | | | |
|---|---|---|---|
| grow | goes | garden | game |
| have | hard | happy | grass |
| January | hot dog | horse | honey |
| king | kick | jar | June |

| | | | |
|---|---|---|---|
| lamb | May | nest | owl |
| ladder | March | morning | October |
| know | love | money | November |
| kite | long | milk | night |

| | | | |
|---|---|---|---|
| prize | sail | shoe | sniff |
| popcorn | ride | shine | smile |
| pond | question | September | slow |
| period | purr | sentence | sister |

| | | | |
|---|---|---|---|
| summer | street | stories | star |
| trip | trick | tail | table |
| when | were | wears | water |
| write | window | wind | where |